Yes There Is Hope

A Parent's Guide to the World of Spina Bifida

Kenida McCormick

Printed in the United States of America

First Printing, 2017

ISBN: 978-1546352341

King James Version Scripture quotations marked
"KJV" are taken from the Holy Bible, King James
Version (Public Domain).

Publishers:
Above The Line Press
McKinney, TX
www.abovethelinepress.com

DEDICATION

To my lovely children Devonte, Deangelo, Destiny, and Desiray, mommy loves you all. Always remember to put God first in all you do, dream big and go for it.

To my wonderful husband, Dustin, thank you for supporting and encouraging me to always believe in myself. Thank you for being my inspiration and most of all my soul mate.

Thanks mom and dad for giving me the tools I needed to become the best mother, wife, friend and mentor I could be. To my brothers and sisters never give up, I love you all. To my Pastor Lorna Taylor, thank you for being a Taylor made pastor, whose smile actually mean "I love you", and whose eyes mean "I'm praying for you". Thank you for being my Jeremiah 3:15. I will continue to make you proud of me. #IHEARGREATER

To my SB family *aka* my Spina Bifida fam, thank you for being a part of my journey. I have a special place in my heart for each and every one of you.#YouguysareAwesome! #YouRock!

A special thank you to the team of doctors and staff members at Duke University Children's Hospital, Lenox Baker Children's Hospital, the

Ronald McDonald House for their help and support with caring for my son Deangelo.

In memory of my baby brother Kalvin Eugene Burr gone but never will be forgotten 10/11/90-5/09/11

TABLE OF CONTENTS

MY LITTLE MESSAGE FROM GOD......................9

THE PURPOSE OF THIS BOOK.........................16

INTRODUCTION TO SPINA BIFIDA....................17

WHAT IS SPINA BIFIDA?. 19

WHAT IS FOLIC ACID?.... 41

SPINA BIFIDA AND TETHERED CORD SYNDROME............45

WHAT IS HYDROCEPHALUS AND SHUNT PLACING?..........51

WHAT IS CHIARI II MALFORMATION?...........................58

EYE PROBLEMS..63

SEIZURES...68

DERMAL SINUS..76

THE URINARY TRACT AND KIDNEYS....................79

HOW SPINA BIFIDA AFFECTS THE BOWEL....................91

WHAT IS A CHAIT CECOSTOMY CATHETER...................102

ORTHOPEDIC AND DEFORMITIES ISSUES....................109

OTHER RELATED MEDICAL ISSUES...........................117

HEALTH CHECK..122

OBESITY...126

DEPRESSION AND ANXIETY............132

AGENT ORANGE BENEFITS ACT............138

LIPOMYELOMENINGOCELE AND LIPOMA............147

WHAT IS SPINAL CORD LIPOMA?...............152

SKIN INTEGRITY BREAKDOWN............159

PRECOCIOUS PUBERTY............165

SEXUAL FUNCTION............171

SCHOOLING FOR KIDS WITH SPINA BIFIDA............178

SOCIAL SKILLS PROBLEM IN KIDS WITH SPINA BIFIDA....190

TRAVELING AND DISABILITIES.. 195

SAFETY............201

GLOSSARY............211

NATIONAL FAMILY RESOURCES............222

MY LITTLE MESSAGE FROM GOD

I grew up the second eldest of seven children, in a small neighborhood in Melbourne, FL. The neighborhood was stricken with drugs and violence. I never really learned what it meant to just be a kid. Unfortunately, I never really learned how to relate to other children being that the oldest sibling was a boy who was rarely home and the rest of my siblings were a lot younger than me.

I was very mature for my age and accustomed to primarily being around adults. Even my own friends and sometimes cousins often annoyed me during my adolescent years. I did well in school, often knowing how to excel beyond my limits, yet self-awareness wasn't something I learned until years later.

I never saw myself having my own family. I didn't want to be tied down to a husband and kids. I always assumed I'd never marry, but that all changed in 1999, when I met my husband Dustin. I agreed to date him after many of my friends and family members pointed out what a great couple we would make. Three years later I became pregnant with my son Devonte.

Two years after Devonte was born I became pregnant with my second child. This pregnancy changed my entire life. Prior to me finding out I was pregnant, God showed me a vision while sitting in the parenting class I was taking at Fayetteville Technical Community College. I signed up for this class as an elective to get my credits towards graduation. I also registered for the class because I wanted to learn more about the different types of parenting skills. I knew it would assist me in raising Devonte. I wanted to be the best mother I could.

The vision began as I was looking through my parenting book and came across an article with a baby that had a sac on its back and I wondered what this big word *Myelomeningocele* labeled beneath the picture meant. I had no clue on how to pronounce the word so I just stared at the picture remembering feeling helpless for the baby and his parents. All of a sudden, it was like my mind went into daydream mode and I saw myself playing with this child from the picture in a bassinet while I laid in the hospital bed and all of my helpless feeling for this child became joy and laughter. I was so happy and at peace.

Then I heard the voice of God say, "This is your child that is within you and one day you will give birth to this little angel." Just like that my daydream was disrupted by the classroom door closing as someone walked in. I nearly jump out of my seat. Trying to reconnect to what was going on in the class and trying to understand what I had just experienced took me for a loop. By the end of class I still couldn't take my mind off of that article so I took the book home to finish reading it. At the conclusion of the article I was so emotionally connected, I did more research on the internet to get a better understanding on this condition.

Two week later, I fell sick. I thought it was the flu because it was flu season. After three days had passed my sickness had not subsided so I went to see my doctor. She ran a variety of test including a pregnancy test. Ten minutes passed as I sat in that cold room wondering what was wrong with me and still trying to make sense of the experience I had two weeks earlier while sitting in class. My doctor walked in with a smile on her face, as she blurted out the words, "you're pregnant, congratulations." The hairs on the back of my neck stood up! I immediately wanted an ultrasound to see how far along I was and to make sure my child was healthy.

On November 23, 2003, I had my first ultrasound to see how far along I was in my pregnancy. My ultrasound showed I was eleven weeks and four days. The sonographer noticed various abnormities with the fetus. I was confused and scared but more than anything I was curious to know more about the abnormities on the ultrasound. I was scheduled to see a specialist for further studies.

Two weeks had passed before I finally saw a specialist. As the specialist conducted my ultrasound he immedialty saw the fetus' abnormities. The specialist noted that my fetus had a lemon shaped Calvarium, Bilateral Ventriculmonegaly, a sac was noted at the Lumbosacral region, Bilateral clubbed feet, four chamber heart with Echogenic Intracardiac Focus (EIF) in the left ventricle of the heart which was all consistent with that one big word I wondered about in my parenting book Myelomeningocele (my-uh-loh-muh-NIN-juh-seel) another word for Spina Bifida. The specialist also found Hydrocephalus (hahy-druh-sef-uh-lus), a buildup of fluid on my fetus brain.

Doctors continued to monitor me until I gave birth by emergency C-section on July 5, 2004. I remember the mood being tense yet joyful at the same time. He was finally here. I didn't get a chance to see him until late that afternoon, because they rushed him straight into surgery. Doctors gently pushed his spinal cord back inside his body through the opening on his back and closed the opening. The following morning doctors would place a shunt into his head to drain the extra fluid off his brain. Doctors gave him three weeks at the most to live because of the severity of his condition.

When I saw my baby for the first time in the ICU unit, hooked up to numerous machines his back wrapped in a special saran wrap to keep infection out, I felt empty inside. The thought of me losing a child that I carried for nine months totally broke my heart. He was lifeless, lying in his bassinet. I hadn't named him because I wanted to see him so that I could give him a befitting name. He was known as Baby Burr, my maiden name at the time.

I sat with him day in and day out and it seemed as though there was no hope. I couldn't hold him. I had to touch him through a small opening on the bassinet due to him being hooked up to so many machines and the high risk of infection. I knew the time was nearing for me to be discharged, and I had to give him a name. As the clock on the wall ticked, I sat and pondered a few names I 'd come across in magazines and books, but none of them seemed to be the perfect fit.

The morning before my discharge the nurse came in and asked if I had picked a name so that they could start the birth certificate process. I told her no because I wanted the perfect name. As she left out the room I said a little prayer to God. I asked him to give me a name that would best fit my baby. An hour passed and my nurse came back in the room, she handed me a book with over five thousand baby names and meanings. I didn't even know where to start, so I figured since my first child name started with a "D" I would look in that section. As I looked through the "D" section I came across Deangelo. I liked it because it had the word angel in it and that fit him quite well. The meaning of Deangelo is "From the Angel " and I knew that was the name that was destined for him.

Today, Deangelo is 12 years old with an incredible sense of humor. His favorite television shows are America's Funniest Home videos and Impractical Jokers. Deangelo can be described by many as unpredictable and strong. He uses a wheelchair or either crutches for mobility. Despite undergoing numerous major surgeries throughout his life he has beat the odds in ways that are unimaginable. That's why I can say to parents with a child that has Spina Bifida or a parent that is expecting a child with Spina Bifida, yes there is hope that lies ahead.

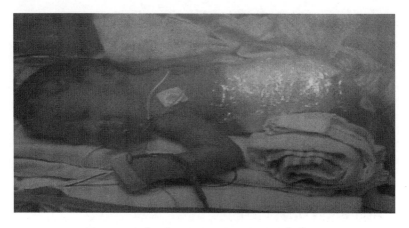

**Deangelo Lamar Mccormick
4 Pounds 13 Ounces**

THE PURPOSE OF THIS BOOK

The purpose of this book is to help give new parents who are expecting a child with Spina Bifida a comprehensive guide to the different challenges they may face when it comes to raising a child with this disability.

The book may also be used to help lift, push and encourage adolescents and adults with Spina Bifida or existing parents raising a child with Spina Bifida. The information and hopeful statements will be the extra push they need in life when they may feel like they are at the point of wanting to give up. I want them to know, at the end of each day that "yes there is hope" through it all.

INTRODUCTION TO SPINA BIFIDA

Spina Bifida is a complex neural tube defect that develops from a small, specialized plate of cells (the neural plate) along the back of an embryo. It is the most devastating of all birth defects. Until the early 1950's babies born with Spina Bifida rarely survived, life expectancy was less than a year. Medical and neurosurgery and urology have changed that.

Those affected require lifelong observation with coordinated management involving the:

- Patient
- Parents
- General Practitioners
- Neurologist
- Physiotherapists
- Occupational Therapists
- Physical Therapists
- Psychologist
- Social Workers
- Speech/Language Pathologist
- Nurses
- Neurosurgeons
- Urologist
- Orthopedic surgeons

- Ophthalmologists
- Orthotists
- Physicians and Other Health Professionals

With this team of coordinators, a person with Spina Bifida is likely to have a more happy active independent life, which may involve being employed and even having children.

CHAPTER 1

WHAT IS SPINA BIFIDA?

Spina Bifida is the most common birth defect in the United States that affects between 1,500 and 2,000 newborns each year. Irish/ English and Hispanic decent have higher rates of Spina Bifida while African Americans have lower rates. The term Spina Bifida is Latin and literally means split or open spine. This process take place before a woman is aware that she is expecting; between 20 to 28 days after conception. It involves the incomplete development in which the backbone and spinal canal of the fetus do not fuse together to cover the spinal cord. This results in the spinal cord and meninges (tissues covering the spinal cord) to protrude from the child's back. Another symptom may include a fluid filled sac surrounding the spinal cord.

To return the spinal cord to its normal position in the spinal canal, surgery is performed under general anesthesia. This helps to prevent further damage and infection to the area, while potentially lessening the amount of tethering or restriction around the spinal cord. The surgery process normally takes one in a half to two hours.

Unfortunately, because of the open spine, the nerves of the spinal cord are damage permanently. A neurosurgeon will determine how much movement, feelings and sensation the baby has by doing a neurological examination. Motor functions are observed by the movement of the muscles and the sensory are determined by different painful stimuli like pin prick or pinch to various areas.

Sometimes it can be very difficult when identifying the exact location of the Spina Bifida. The different degree of muscle paralysis varies in each child. A healthy spine is closed to protect the spinal cord which is a bundle of nerves that send messages back and forth between your brain and the rest of your body. The point in which the Spina Bifida is affected is called the level. The higher or lower the level is determines the severity of each malformation case. Myelomeningocele is the most serve case. Some children with Spina Bifida will be ambulatory. This is why few children with the disease walk without assistance, while others will walk using crutches, a walker, little or no bracing or use a wheelchair.

Once a couple has one child with this birth defect, their risk of having a second child with the defect increases 1 to 5 out of 100. Up to 95 percent of babies born with Spina Bifida and other neural tube defects are born to parents with no family history of these disorders. The life expectancy for children with Spina Bifida has changed over the years. Studies show that with the proper medical care at least 75% of children with the most severe case will live well into early adulthood.

Symptoms of Spina Bifida:

- Abnormal appearance of the baby's back, varying from a small, hairy patch, dimple or birthmark, to sac-like protrusion that is found along the back bone area.
- Bowel and bladder problems (constipation, incontinence)
- Loss of feeling below the area of the lesion, especially in babies born with a meningocele or myelomeningocele.
- Inability to move the lower legs (paralysis)
- Partial or complete lack of sensation
- Hydrocephalus (increase fluids and pressure in the head area; occurs in about 80 to 90 percent of cases)
- Orthopedic (bone) problems like weakness of the hips, legs, or feet.
- Subtle learning problems
- Epilepsy and seizures
- Skin issues (Such as pressure ulcers or

injuries) resulting from decrease sensation.
- Strabismus (sometimes called lazy eye)
- Weight gain

Different malformation cases of Spina Bifida:

- **Spina Bifida Occulta**- The mildest and most common form of Spina Bifida. There are one or more vertebrae that are malformed. The spinal cords and nerves are usually normal, and most affected individuals need no treatment. Occulta is a word that means hidden and indicates that a layer of skin covers the malformation, or opening of the spine. This form of Spina Bifida rarely causes a disability or symptoms, and is present in 10 to 20 percent of the general population. A few have a hairy patch, dark spot, dimple or swelling over the affected area.

- **Closed neural tube defects**-This form consist of a diverse group of defects in which the spinal cord is marked by malformation of fat, bone, or meninges. In some people it causes few to no symptoms but other might experience partial paralysis or other symptoms with the urinary and bowel dysfunction.

- **Meningocele**- (mun-NUN-juh-seel). In meningocele the spinal fluids and meninges protrude from the spinal opening and the malformation may or may be covered by a layer of skin or cyst. The cyst is removed by surgery. Some people with meningocele may have few to no symptoms while others may experience symptoms more severe similar to those of closed neural tube defect.

- **Myelomeningocele**- (my-uh-loh-muh-NIN-juh-seel). This Spina Bifida is the most severe form of them all. There is a lot of damage done to the nervous system bones, muscles, kidneys and the bladder due to the nerves being exposed throughout the pregnancy. Affected babies are at high risk of infection until the back is closed. Paralysis and incontinence of bowel and bladder may occur frequently not cured by surgery. Many babies born with this type of Spina Bifida also have hydrocephalus, a buildup of fluids in the brain that increase pressure on the brain.

This chart gives you a simple look of the nerves and disabilities at different levels of the spine:

Cervical Region

Begins	**Nerves that may be affected**
C-5	Elbow flexors: Partial extremity function
C-6	Wrist extensors: Standing with stander/orthotics
C-7	Elbow extenders
C-8	Finger flexors

Thoracic Region

Begins	Nerves that may be affected
T-2	Complete upper extremity function
T-3 to T-8	Standing with stander/orthotics
T-4	Possible exercise ambulation
T-7	Partial function of the trunk muscles
T-9 toT-12	Exercise ambulation
T-10 to L-2	Bladder: Sympathetic input from hypogastric nerve
T-11	Some function of the trunk
T-12 to S-5	Sexual function varies

Lumber Region

Begins	**Nerves that may be affected**
L-1	Complete trunk function: exercise ambulation Sometimes household ambulation
L-2	Hip flexor muscles present: exercise ambulation Household ambulation
L-3	Knee extensors or Quadriceps muscles present: Household ambulation possible community ambulation, possible community ambulation
L-4	Medial Knee flexors present. Ankle dorsiflexors 3/5 strength
L-5	May walk with or without braces crutches in home

Sacral Region

Begins	Nerves that may be affected
S-1	Hip abductors, 3/5 strength.
S-2	Hip extensors, 4/5 strength. Ankle, plantarflexors, 3/5 strength. May walk with or without crutches
S-2 to S-4	Bowel and bladder function varies. Bladder: Parasymapathetic input from the pelvic nerve. Somatic input from pudendal nerve to urethral sphincter.
S-3	All muscle activity may be within normal limits.
S-5 and above	Be aware of the signs of the shunt malfunction and tethered spinal cord.

Tests Associated with Spina Bifida:

- Computerized tomography (CT)

- Cystometrogram/Electromyogram (CMG/EMG)

- Voiding cystourethrogram

- Magnetic resonance imaging (MRI)

- Ultrasonography

- X-ray

- Manual muscle testing

- Neuropsychological evaluations

Yes There Is Hope!

For me, Spina Bifida has been a challenge but I take it in strides, one day at a time! Spina Bifida is a unique birth defect that is different in each person. Each case of Spina Bifida is like a snowflake with very unique qualities. What works for one person may not for another. Spina Bifida is hard to accept in a world that sees different is wrong. I believe the hardest part of Spina Bifida, is the loss of feeling in parts of the body and having a hard time getting the bathroom side of things down packed. -Jen Evans

I would say, to any parent of an only child with Spina Bifida, give them room to spread their wings and fly. Don't overprotect, because your child will amaze you. Let life happen. - Bethany Fields

I wouldn't be able to get through life without God and the strength He gives me. With God all things are possible! (Matthew 19:26) I can do all things through him who gives me strength! (Philippians 4:13) -Summer Conner

Having Spina Bifida isn't an end; it's a new beginning. Just because I have Spina Bifida doesn't mean it has me or ever will. No one dictates what I can do. I am my own independent married woman who lives life the best possible thanks to Spina Bifida. It's not a disability unless I make it one; it's just a different ability. -Ruth Eliana Cleveland-Mott

My child is the fifth consecutive generation of our family to have a Spina Bifida diagnosis. She has was diagnosed with Spina Bifida Occulta with Myelomeningocele symptoms complicated by tethered cord and three tumors located inside the spinal cord itself, making surgery very risky. She is the light of our lives and one of the happiest kids you will ever meet. Spina Bifida will not stop her from achieving anything she wants out of life. She is our champion, beating the Bif! -Alison Ross

Rejoice always, pray without ceasing, and give thanks in all circumstances; for this is the will of God in Christ Jesus for you. (1Thessalonians 5:16) -Anjule Sara Cooper

Don't feel like the world is ending, miracles happen! Cherish the little battles you're fighting and winning every day! I'm the aunt to the sweetest and strongest little fighter I've ever met. He shows us if it's meant to be, it will. With less than a 5% chance of making it into the world my

nephew has fought to stay. Every baby is a blessing the special ones are miracles the rest of us get to enjoy. -Sarah Dunmire

I'm very fortunate because my daughter's condition isn't as severe as others. If I could give advice to a parent who was in my shoes almost two years ago it would be this, don't listen to the Doctor's before your child arrives. There are several things the specialists told us my daughter would never do that she's done. Let your children tell you what they can and can't do. Also, don't be afraid to speak up for your child. You are their biggest advocate in this world. No one will fight for them as hard as you can and will. -Shiloh Abner

As an aunt of a little boy with Spina Bifida I would say treat them no different from anyone else and love them unconditionally.-Tequila Johnson Garcia

The bible says (Philippians 4:13) I can do all things through Christ who strengthens me. For 37 years that scripture has reminded me that my capabilities aren't in my disability or me, it's in God. -Johnny Edward Patton Jr.

Latex allergies in people with Spina Bifida

Latex is rubber that has been manufactured from the sap of the Hevea Brasiliensis (a rubber tree). The sap is mixed with chemicals during manufacturing to give latex it elastic quality. Latex can be found in many household hospital and community items. Research studies have shown that approximately 76% of babies and adolescents with Spina Bifida are at high risk for developing a latex allergy due to exposure to a protein found in latex from medical products such as, gloves used in multiple surgical procedures, diagnostic test, examination and bladder and bowel programs early in the child's life.

Latex allergy occurs when the body's natural defenses against an allergen are threatened. It involves the production of antibodies when there is contact with a specific antigen in this case latex. Your body treats latex as an allergen and sets off an allergic reaction. Symptoms can range from mild to severe depending on the degree of sensitivity and the amount latex allergen to which you are exposed. The most serious allergic reaction to latex is anaphylactic (an-uh-fuh-LAK-tik) response, which can be deadly. It's rarely the first reaction to latex exposure. Anaphylactic reactions develop immediately after latex exposure in highly sensitive people.

Certain fruits and vegetables such as avocados, bananas, chestnuts, kiwis and passion fruits can cause allergic symptoms in some latex sensitive individuals. Precautions are taken by the healthcare team to reduce the baby's exposure to products that contain latex. Your baby's healthcare providers can help you identify products that contain latex and also find products that are latex-free.

Mild latex allergy symptoms

- Rash
- Itching of the skin
- Skin redness
- Hives

More severe latex allergy symptoms:

- Swollen eyes
- Swelling of the skin
- Itchy skin
- Chest tightness
- Runny nose
- Sneezing
- Itchy watery eyes
- Scratchy throat
- Breathing difficulty

- Wheezing
- Cough
- Light headedness
- Fainting

People who are at risk for latex allergy:

- Children with Spina Bifida
- Children who have had many surgeries
- Children born with anomalies of the urinary system

Anaphylactic response to latex signs and symptoms:

- Difficulty breathing caused by swelling of the lips tongue and windpipe.
- Severe wheezing
- Severe drop in blood pressure (hypotension)
- Dizziness
- Loss of consciousness
- Confusion
- Slurred speech
- Rapid or weak pulse
- Diarrhea
- Nausea and vomiting

- Blue hue of the skin, including lips and nails beds

Common foods that contain same protein as latex:

- Bananas
- Avocados
- Chestnuts
- Kiwi
- Passion fruit
- Papaya
- Nectarines
- Plums
- Tomatoes
- Celery
- Mangoes
- Potatoes

Some Household and Community/Hospital products that contain latex:

- Eye dropper Bulbs
- Catheters
- Elastic bandages
- IV tubing injecting site
- Household gloves
- Hospital gloves

- Condoms, diaphragms
- Catheters
- Condom incontinence aids
- Dental products (such as mouth guards)
- Adhesive tapes (sticky plasters)
- Some urinary catheters
- Some enema tubing
- Protective sheets
- Colostomy/urostomy products
- Balloons (including mylar) Koosh ball and rubber balls
- Art supplies
- Dental dams
- Baby bottles, nipples, pacifiers
- Elastic on clothes
- Beach toys
- Chewing gum
- Electrode pads
- Rubber bands
- Bands aids
- Erasers
- Hand grips on racquets and bicycles
- Wheelchair tires
- Blood pressure cuffs
- Tourniquets
- Stethoscopes

- Sport shoes and rubber clothing (such as raincoats)
- Disposable diapers
- Chux (waterproof pads)

Latex precautions:

- Avoid contact with natural rubber latex products. Substitutes are available for most commonly used items.

- Let your doctor, surgeon or dentist know about your allergy before your appointment. If you can be scheduled first this will again minimize the risk of exposure to airborne particles.

- Check your place of work or school. Let them know so they can replace equipment and products used with non-latex substitutes.

- Consult your doctor about medicine you can take to reduce the allergy symptoms.

- Be aware that some people are allergic to latex also shows allergies to certain foods, especially bananas and avocados.

- Use a Medic-Alert Bracelet or necklace.

- Avoid all Latex products at home and in hospital. Use items that do not have latex in them.

- Know what to do in case of emergency.

Yes There Is Hope!

Always keep going no matter what. -Anna Adams

I had so many doubts and was convinced that the worst was bound to happen, but now that I've seen that the children can be happy and live normal lives I can finally breathe. -Cody McFadden

I can say as a Grandparent I've never seen my grandson's disability stop him from doing what he wants to do. He has encouraged me because he is independent and he doesn't want anyone to do anything for him. -Eunice Freeman

Even though my nephew has Spina Bifida he has a strong will power and strong courage to enjoy life. -Freddrick Burr

It could always be worse. -Zac Cannady

Treat your child as if they weren't disabled. You will be amazed at what we can do when labels don't hold us back. -Monica Stills

People with Spina Bifida are some of the toughest people around. They can also amaze you every day with what they can do. It's really awesome when it is something you are told by doctors they won't ever be able to do! Every person's case is different and unique. -Leanne Johnson

Fetal surgery and bed rest at the time were so hard, but after seeing my precious baby that is now overcoming so many milestones that the doctors said she never would, it was "ALL" worth it. Keep your faith, pray daily, and no matter what, God will never give you anything that you can't handle! -Meriah Christine Murphy

A diagnosis of Spina Bifida sometimes takes away from the fact that you've still got a beautiful baby waiting to meet you. After your child is born, all you notice is her smile, her eyes, her perfect skin and little nose. Spina Bifida becomes secondary. -Kimmy Lynch

My favorite bible verse is "Delight thyself also in the Lord; and He shall give thee the desires of thine heart." (Psalm 37:4) -Glennaye McMillian Sloan

CHAPTER 2

WHAT IS FOLIC ACID?

Studies that were conducted with mothers who have had prior Spina Bifida births indicated that the incidence of Spina Bifida could be decreased by up to 70% when the mother takes a daily dose of vitamin B (folic acid) supplement prior to conception, and at least 3 months after. The Vitamin B is believed to help in the closing of the spinal tube and potentially reduce the risk of having a fetus with the neural tube defect. That is why it is very important for all women of childbearing age especially those who are planning pregnancy to consume about 400 micrograms (0.4 milligrams) of folic acid every day. This vitamin is 100% recommended daily allowance and can be found over the counter multivitamin supplement section in most drugs stores.

Eating green foods such as vegetables, pastas, fruits and juices boosts your intake Folic acid naturally. A lot of cereal, breads and rice have folic acid as well. Unfortunately, most people do not get enough through food alone. The best way to get the right amount of folic acid is to eat a healthy diet or take a Multi vitamin B pill daily.

Yes There Is Hope!

If I could say anything to parents with Spina Bifida children or those expecting a child with Spina Bifida, it would be, when doctors give prognosis, God already has a plan. -Scott Hall

Never give up. Be strong and keep trying to be the best that you can! -Kevin Dagostino

By the grace of God I believe that a child with Spina Bifida male or female if they have good loving parents and believe in the good Lord above, they too shall accomplish anything. - Debbie J. Alexander

I'm a 43 year Spina Bifida WARRIOR! I truly have faith if I can make it in the 70s-80s your child can too. -Billy Winneroski

I have Spina Bifida; Spina Bifida does not have me. Live a full life and be the absolute best you can be. -Greg Kornnacki

Overcoming obstacles may not be easy but it can be done. Never give up. -Jackie Fleury

No matter how bad things might look there is someone that has it worse! This too shall pass. - Angel Jatko

Always follow your instincts! Don't let people, places, or things stop you or your child from enjoying every day things; treat them like any other child. -Keagan Kertcher

"I'm not disabled, I'm differently-able. Don't judge me for what I can or can't do, but judge me for my character, morals, and integrity instead. - Laura Eckstein

Always think positive don't let anything sink you so low you can't get back up. -Richie Souza

CHAPTER 3

SPINA BIFIDA AND TETHERED CORD SYNDROME

Tethered Cord Syndrome is a neurological disorder caused by tissue attachments that limit the movement of the spinal cord within the spinal column. Attachments may occur congenitally at the base of the spinal cord (conus medillaris) or they may develop near the site of an injury to the spinal cord. These attachments cause an abnormal stretching of the spinal cord, resulting in decreased blood flow to the spinal cord and nerves. The course of the disorder is progressive. In children, symptoms may include lesions, hairy patches, dimples, or fatty tumors on the lower back; foot and spinal deformities; weakness in the leg; low back pain; scoliosis; and incontinence. This type of tethered spinal cord syndrome appears to be the result of improper growth of the neural tube during fetal development, and is closely linked to Spina Bifida.

Tethered spinal cord syndrome may go undiagnosed until adulthood, when pain, sensory and motor problems, loss of bowel and bladder control develops. This delayed presentation of symptoms is related to the degree of strain placed on the spinal column (stenosis) with age. Tethering may develop after spinal cord injury and scar tissue can block the flow of fluids around the spinal cord. Fluid pressure may cause cysts to form in the spinal cord, a condition called syringomyelia. This can lead to additional loss of movement, feeling or the onset of pain or autonomic symptoms.

Symptoms of tethered cord:

- Lesion on lower back
- Spine tenderness
- Fatty tumor or deep dimple on the lower back
- Leg numbness or tingling
- Leg deformities
- Hairy patch on the lower back
- Changes in leg strength
- Progressive or repeated muscle contraction
- Scoliosis (curvature of the spine)
- Skin discoloration on the lower back
- Deterioration in gait
- Bowel and bladder problems
- Leg pain, especially in the back of leg
- Back pain, worsened by activity and relieved with rest

Other causes of tethered cord:

- A history of spine surgery
- Dermal sinus track (a rare congenital deformity)
- Tumor
- Diastematomyelia (spilt spinal cord)
- A history of spine trauma
- Lipoma (a benign, fatty growth)
- Thickened/tight filum terminale (a delicate filament near the tailbone)

Difficulties with tethered cord:

- Back pain
- Leg pain
- Weakness or numbness in the legs and feet
- Difficulty standing or walking
- Fecal and/or urinary incontinence

Different forms of tethered cord:

- Tight filum terminale
- Lipomeningomyelocele
- Split cord malformation (diastematomyelia)
- Dermal sinus tracts
- Dermoids
- Cystoceles

Tethered cord tests that are performed:

- Magnetic Resonance Imaging (MRI)
- Myleogram
- CT or CAT scan
- Ultrasound
- Manual Muscles Test (MMT)
- Spine X-rays
- Cystometrogram CGM

Tethered cord treatment:

To free the spinal cord, neurosurgeons first do a procedure called a Laminectomy, then the neurosurgeon frees up the spinal cord by gently cutting, or teasing, it away from the scar tissue or fat. After the spinal cord is free, neurosurgeons sometimes apply a patch to cover the spinal cord (duramater). This limits the chances that cerebrospinal fluids (CSF) will leak.

Yes There Is Hope!

"Love conquers all." -Jennifer Pritchard's

"My favorite quote by an author, "Don't dis my ability." -Nicole Wetly

"Dr. Seuss said, "Why fit in, when you were born to stand out." -Sarah Ruiz

"Many have been told some devastating things about their kids born with Spina Bifida but encouragement, understanding patience and love is what gives anyone born with Spina Bifida a chance to soar. My son was told he would never walk and he was going to be mentally challenged but God knows best and now he walks, even runs, with no assistance and has been reading since the age of 2. In his words he says everyday, Mommy I love my life." - Stephanie Patterson Williams

"My favorite quote is by Author Ernesto Che Guevar, Live your life not celebrating victories, by overcoming defeats." -Mijesh Markose

"You have Spina Bifida. Spina Bifida doesn't have you." -Jo Ellen Bonham's

"I always sing this lyric to my three year old soon to be four, Get over your hill and see what

you find there, with grace in your heart and flowers in your hair." -Sara Abute

"Be yourself and try not to be afraid." - Hilary Hauschild

"My favorite bible verses are, "Before I shaped you in the womb, I knew all about you. Before you saw the light of day, I had holy plans for you."(Jeremiah 1:5) For I knew the plans I have declares the Lord, plans to prosper you and not harm you plans to give a hope and a future. (Jeremiah 29:11)" -Lachelle Balensiefen

"My favorite quote is by Author David Icke, The greatest prison people live in is fear of what other people think." -Matthew C. Coker

CHAPTER 4

WHAT IS HYDROCEPHALUS AND SHUNT PLACING?

The term Hydrocephalus comes from the Greek words "Hydro" meaning water and "cephalous" meaning head. It is a condition in which the cerebrospinal fluid blocks the flow of fluids, which normally move in and around the brain, and results in abnormal collection of fluid within the cavities or ventricles of the brain. These ventricles expand from the fluid putting potentially harmful pressure on the surrounding brain tissue; 80% - 90% of children with Spina Bifida will develop hydrocephalus. Hydrocephalus is found on prenatal ultrasound testing in most infants with the myelomeningocele form of Spina Bifida.

This is corrected through a surgery by placing a shunt which is a long thin soft plastic flexible tube in the fluid filled spaces in the brain that extend to the abdomen which helps to drain the excess fluid. The fluid then goes back into the blood where it properly belongs. Shunts are named according to where they are places in the brain to drain the excess fluid out. People cannot tell you have a shunt just by looking at you. The shunt is placed under the skin; 95% of the people with Spina Bifida have hydrocephalus and a shunt.

Even though the reliability of shunts has improved since the early centuries, they are devices that can fail. Sometimes they are out grown and can come apart if too short or become clogged at either end. The sign and symptoms of the shunt not working vary with age and from person to person. If you are having problems call your doctor or your neurosurgeon. A neurosurgeon is a surgeon who operates on the spinal cord and the brain that will do surgery to fix the problem. Respond quickly to the signs the shunt is not properly operating. It can be repaired or even replaced but going without fixing the problem may result in death.

Sign of shunt malfunction:

Infants
- Enlarged head size
- Full or Bulging fontanel (soft spot)
- Prominent scalp veins
- Swelling along the shunt track
- Vomiting
- Irritability

- Sleepiness
- Eyes looking downward
- Less interest in eating
- Crossed eyes (new or worsening)

Toddlers
- Increase in head size
- Vomiting
- Headache
- Irritability
- Sleepiness
- Swelling along shunt track
- Crossed eyes
- Loss of previous abilities (sensory or motor function)

Children and adults
- Vomiting
- Headache
- Vision problem
- Personality change
- Deterioration in school/Job performance
- Loss of coordination or balance
- Pain in Spina Bifida repair site
- Swelling along the shunt track
- Difficulty in waking up or staying awake
- Decline in academic performance

Less common signs of shunt problems:
- Seizures (either the onset of new seizures or increase in the frequency of existing seizures).

- Back pain at the Spina Bifida closure site.
- Worsening arm or leg function (increasing weakness or loss of sensation, worsening orthopedic deformities).
- Increase scoliosis
- Worsening speech or swallowing difficulties.
- Changes in the bowel or bowel function

Different parts of a Shunt:

Upper Catheter- The top-most part of the shunt that reaches the area around the brain where there is excess cerebrospinal fluid.

Valve-The valve is used to regulate the flow of the cerebrospinal fluid.

Reservoir- this is known as the flushing chamber where excess cerebrospinal fluid is collected and is drained to the bottom portion of the shunt. Also used for doctors to collect samples of the cerebrospinal fluid for testing and injecting fluid in to test the flow of fluid and measure the pressure to make sure it's working properly.

Lower Catheter- The bottom-most part of the shunt that carries the excess cerebrospinal fluid from one part of the body to the other such as the abdomen (belly) or the heart.

Different shunt systems:

Shunt Pathway	Shunt Type CFS	Inflow Location CSF	Drainage Location
Ventriculo - gall bladder	VGB	Ventricle	Gall Bladder
Ventriculo - peritoneal	VP	Ventricle	Peritoneal cavity
Ventriculo - atrial	VA	Ventricle	Right atrium of the heart
Ventriculo - pleural	VPL	Ventricle	Pleural cavity
Lumbo - peritoneal	LP	Lumber spine	Peritoneal cavity

Yes There Is Hope!

Keep moving forward. —Danielle Thomas George

My Spina Bifida superhero has changed the way I view the entire world for the better! -Liz Bennett Potter

My favorite quote is by Paulo Coelho, "It's not your business what other people think about you." -Gale Bommen Goldberg

My favorite Bible verses are: But those who hope in the Lord will renew their strength. They will soar on wings like eagles; they will run and not grow weary, they will walk and not faint. (Isaiah 40:31) I can do all things through Christ, which strengthens me! (Philippians 4:13) -Kim McBride

Put your trust in God Not Google. -Melinda Beckmann

We as people with Spina Bifida come along way with positive people in our lives and have family that help us grow and care for ourselves but would help if we need it. -Timothy Calixo

My favorite quote is by Author Scott Hamilton, "The only disability in life is a bad attitude." -Chrissy Stines

My favorite bible verse is, With God all things are possible. (Matthew 19:26) Because He Lives is my favorite song to sing. -Becky Covington

I always remind myself of two things, one, Evie is fearfully and wonderfully made perfectly by our creator and two, the combination of love, therapy, science and the grace and healing powers of Jesus Christ makes the impossible possible. -Heather Morgan

My favorite bible verse is I will praise you, for I am fearfully and wonderfully made, marvelous are your works, and that my soul knows very well. (Psalm 139:14) -Meaghann Malone

CHAPTER 5

WHAT IS CHIARI II MALFORMATION?

When part of the cerebellum is located below the foramen magnum, it is called the Chiari ll Malformation. The brains of most children with open Spina Bifida are positioned abnormally. The lower part of the brain rests farther down than normal, partially in the upper spinal canal. The cerebrospinal (pronounced suh-ree-broh-SPAHYN-L) fluid can get block and cause hydrocephalus.

While most affected children have no symptoms, a few may have upper body weakness and trouble breathing and swallowing. Chiari ll Malformation affects females more often than males. There are four types of Chiari ll Malformation. Type 2 is the most common in children with Spina Bifida.

Symptoms of Chiari ll Malformation:

- Dizziness
- Muscle weakness
- Swallowing difficulties

- Breathing irregularities
- Changes in nerve function in the throat or tongue
- Headaches made worse by coughing or sneezing
- Speech problems
- Pain in lower back of the head into the neck
- Sleep Apnea
- Vision problems (blurred or double vision)
- Headaches
- Problems with balance and coordination/poor hand coordination
- Numbness and tingling of the hands and feet
- Ringing or buzzing in the ears

Different types of Chiari ll Malformation:

- Type1: The most common in children. In this type is the lower part of the cerebellum but not the brain stem extends into an opening at the base of the skull. This type is the only one that can be acquired.

- Type2: Also known as "classic" Chiari malformation or Arnold-Chiari malformation. Occurs when both the tissue from the cerebellum, along with the brain stem itself, extends into the foramen magnum. This is usually only seen at birth in children born with Spina Bifida.

- Type3: The most serious but rare form of Chiari Malformation. It involves the cerebellum and brain stem that produce a pouch –like structure that protrudes from the foramen magnum and into the spinal cord. This usually cause severe neurological defects.

- Type4: A rare type that involves and incomplete or undeveloped cerebellum. Its Sometimes is associated with exposed parts of the skull and spinal cord.

Treatment for Chiari ll Malformation:

- Balance
- Touch
- Reflexes
- Sensation
- Motor skills

Testing done for Chiari ll Malformation:

- X-ray
- MRI
- CT scan
- Laryngoscopy

Yes There Is Hope!

Life isn't all about what you don't have, but yet, what you do with what you have been given. -Stephanie L. Stanley

"Scars are medals made of skin they show how very brave you are."-Jordan Page Crownover.

I always say Anika has Spina Bifida but Spina Bifida will never have her. She is fearfully and wonderfully made. -Annel Greyling Strydom

Don't let your diagnosis define you. My daughter is so full of life and abilities. -Heather Weir

"Doctors are not prophets; they can't see into the future. Therefore, doctors can't accurately predict what the life of a person with Spina Bifida will be like!"-Julie Gibson Elander

We were told my son would never have a good life but now he is 18, made the honor roll, play sports, goes to school and lives a full life. Kids with Spina Bifida will amaze you. -Donna Strom

The power of God, positive encouragement and your child will determine what he/she will do. Never let a doctor, therapist or anyone put limits on your little miracle! -Alisha Eads

My favorite bible verse is, "I can do all things through Christ who strengthens me." (Philippians 4:13) -Noel Fugett

The day after our daughter's diagnosis with Spina Bifida, I was on the couch, back to the world, with tears freely flowing. I was deeply grieving the baby I thought I was pregnant with, before finding out there were abnormalities at our ultrasound. I'll forever credit my husband for saving me, and I'll never forget him sitting down next to me and saying these words: "Cheer up Charlie, his nickname for me. This isn't the end of the world. I knew in that second we would get through this and do it together. That was three years ago, and we're rocking the whole special needs parent thing if I do say so myself! -Kristen Slone

It's just a disability don't let it hinder or define who you are as a person. Show the world disabled people can do anything and everything we put our minds to. -Nathan Reno

CHAPTER 6

EYE PROBLEMS

Eye problems may be the first sign of raised pressure in the brain, hydrocephalus or shunt blockage can cause pressure around the brain which can also produce pressure on the optic nerve and lead to poor vision, so it is important to monitor the eyes. Visual information is transmitted to the brain by the optic nerve, a cord that runs from the eye to the brain. The meninges that surround the brain and spinal cord also surround the optic nerve. Visual assessments and ocular assessments, which monitor eye movements and examine the back of the eye, are recommended.

There is a high incidence of eye problems in patients with hydrocephalus, such as strabismus (squint or lazy eye) is a common disorder in 3 to 4 percent of children in the general population but is even more common in those with Spina Bifida. Without early treatment vision may be permanently impaired. If strabismus does not go away in the first six months of life it is recommended a pediatric ophthalmologist (eye specialist) evaluate the infant. Shunt failure may cause new strabismus or worsening of an existing condition.

Other conditions of the eyes and vision:

- Cerebral Visual impairment (CVI)
- Visual Field Loss
- Optic Atrophy
- Nystagmus

Treatment:

- Placing a patch over the dominant eye
- Surgery to help align the eye muscles

Yes There Is Hope!

My favorite bible verse is "For I know the plans I have for you," declares the Lord, "plans to prosper you and not to harm you, plans to give you hope and future. (Jeremiah 29:11) -Cole Watkins

My favorite bible verse is "Before I formed you in the womb I knew you, before you were born I set you apart; appointed you as a prophet to the nations." (Jeremiah 1:5) -Darlene Woodham Watkins

If God brings you to it...he will bring you through it! -Lisa Penn

You don't have to feel sorry for my daughters. Wheelchairs give them freedom and their life is full of love and joy. They never miss out on anything! -Author Jamie Lynn Veprek

"For every weakness, there is a greater strength. -Shannon Riebe's favorite quote by Author Jean Driscoll

"If the life of a man or woman on earth is to bear the fragrance of heaven the winds of God must blow on that life, winds not always balmy from the south, but fierce winds from the north that chill the very marrow." -Shelly Ross favorite

quote by Author Elisabeth Elliot

My go-to bible verses are: Therefore being justified by faith, we have peace with God through our Lord Jesus Christ: By whom also we have access by faith into this grace wherein we stand, and rejoice in hope of the glory of God. And not only so, but we glory in tribulations also: knowing that tribulations worketh patience; And patience, experience; and experience, hope: And hope maketh not ashamed; because the love of God is shed abroad in our hearts by the Holy Ghost which is given unto us. (Romans 5:1-5) Finally, brethren, whatsoever things are true, whatsoever things are honest, whatsoever things are just, whatsoever things are pure, whatsoever things are lovely, whatsoever things are of good report; if there be any virtue, and if there be any praise, think on those things. (Philippians 4:8) Don't live in the past or you may live in regret. Don't live in the future or you will be anxious. Live in the moment; keep your head where your feet are. – Cindi Byron-Dixion's go to bible verse and favorite quote by Author Kevin Kling

My favorite bible verse is, "I can do all things through Christ that strengthens me." (Philippians 4:13) -Natasha Edwards

My favorite bible verse is "But now, this is what the Lord says-He created you, Jacob, He who formed you, Israel: 'Do not fear, for I have redeemed you; I have summoned you by name you are mine. When you pass though the waters, I will be with you; and when you pass through the rivers, they will not sweep over you. When you walk through the fire, you will not be burned; the flames will not set you ablaze. For I am the Lord your God, the Holy One of Israel, your Savior; I give Egypt for your ransom, Crush and Seba in your stead. (Isaiah 43:1-3) I love this passage because it not only tells us that there will be trials in our lives and we will have hardships, but that we will not be defeated through them. "They WILL NOT sweep over you... the flames WILL NOT set you ablaze." It is just so comforting. -Sarah Alley

I don't consider my daughter disabled. However, she was born with a short right arm. It did not develop past her elbow. I discovered this poem called "Welcome to Holland" when I was pregnant with her and it helped me. -Ashley Catharine

CHAPTER 7

SEIZURES

Seizures are changes in the brain's electrical activity. This can cause dramatic, noticeable symptoms or even no symptoms at all. A seizure may be a one-time event or you may have seizures repeatedly. Less than 1 in 10 people who have had a seizure develop epilepsy.

Seizures (epilepsy) occur in approximately 1 in every 500 children in the United States. The figure rises to about 1 in 20 with Spina Bifida. The risk of developing a seizure disorder is greatest for those who have had central nervous system infections, have had their shunt fail a number of times, or have had episodes of respiratory insufficiency or arrest. Most seizure disorders are successfully treated with medication.

The symptoms of a severe seizure are often widely recognized, including violent shaking and loss of control. However, mild seizures can also be a sign of a significant medical problem, so recognizing them is important. Since some seizures can lead to injury or be evidence of an underlying medical condition, it is important to seek treatment if you experience them.

The most common type of seizures:

Generalized Seizure: (entire brain)	Symptoms
Grand Mal or Generalized tonic-clonic	Unconsciousness, convulsion, muscle rigidity
Absence	Brief lost of consciousness
Myoclonic	Sporadic (isolated), jerking movements
Clonic	Repetitive, jerking movement
Tonic	Muscle stiffness, rigidity
Atonic	Loss of muscle tone

Partial seizures: (small area of the brain)	**Symptoms**
Simple (awareness is retained)	
Simple Motor	Jerking, muscle rigidity, spasms, head-turning
Simple Sensory	Unusual sensation affecting either the vision, hearing, smell taste, or touch
Simple Psychological	Memory or emotional disturbances
Complex (Impairment of awareness)	Automatisms such as lip smacking, chewing, fidgeting, walking and other repetitive, involuntary but coordinated movements

Partial seizure with secondary generalization	Symptoms that are initially associated with a preservation of consciousness that then evolves into a loss of consciousness and convulsion

Warning signs and symptoms of a seizure:

- Sudden feelings of fear or anxiousness
- Feeling sick to your stomach
- Dizziness
- A change in vision
- A blackout of time, followed by confusion
- Uncontrollable muscle spasms
- Drooling or frothing at the mouth
- Falling
- Experiencing a strange taste in your mouth
- Clenching teeth
- Sudden, rapid eye movements
- Making unusual noises, such as grunting
- Losing control of bladder or bowel function
- Sudden mood changes

Things that causes seizures:

- Alcohol withdrawal
- Bites and/or stings
- Brain infection, such as meningitis
- Brain injury during childbirth
- Brain defect present at birth
- Brain tumor
- Choking
- Cancer
- Drug abuse
- Drug withdrawals
- Electrolyte imbalance
- Electric shock

- Epilepsy
- Extremely high blood pressure
- Fever
- Head trauma
- Kidney or liver failure
- Low blood glucose levels
- Medications, such as antipsychotics and some asthma drugs
- Repetitive sound or flashing lights, such as in video games
- Stroke
- Use of drugs such as cocaine and heroin
- Withdrawal from medications, such as Xanax or narcotics

Yes There Is Hope!

My quote is from my favorite childhood cartoon, Transformers, "More than meets the eye." I choose this because it challenge people to not underestimate those with disabilities and it challenges those with disabilities to break the expectations of those observing them. -Dan S. Simken Jr.

Never give up when God is ready he will take him, fight the good fight. -Cristina Brammer

Without my Country Concerts I go too, I don't think I could even deal with Spina Bifida. -Lauren DeShields

My favorite quote is by an author unknown, "Don't tell God how big your mountain is; tell your mountain how big God is." -Lisa Neufeld

Prayer helps and reading "Heaven Is For Real" got me through and when I have doubts I read it again. -Jerry Mejeur

My favorite quote is by Author Scott Hamilton, "The only disability is a bad attitude." -Alvaro Othsmaro

I can reach the stars too, I just reach them different and that's okay. -Sue Ellen Warren

I have abilities with an inconvenience. -Lovelle Faith

My favorite bible verse is, "I can do all things through Christ who strengthens me." (Philippians 4:13) -Chrissy Stines

My favorite bible verse is, "Delight yourself in the Lord, and He shall grant you the desires of your heart." (Psalm 37:4) -Patricia Jaramillo

CHAPTER 8

DERMAL SINUS

Some babies with myelomeningocele may develop meningitis, an infection in the tissues surrounding the brain, which are life-threatening due to the fact that they may cause brain injury. Dermal sinus refers to a pathway covered in skin, which stretches from a small pit on the surface of the back to the deeper structures. There it extends all the way to the spinal canal, passes through the spinal meninges and is usually anchored to the conus (the bottom end) of the spinal cord. Affected children may become prone to meningitis through this sinus because there is a direct connection to the cerebrospinal fluid. For this reason, an operation maybe necessary in which the pathway is followed to its fixation point on the spinal cord is separated and completely removed.

Symptoms of Dermal Sinus:

- A spinal dermal sinus may appear as a dimple or sinus (open tract), with or without hairs, usually very close to the midline, with an opening of only 1 to 2 millimeters. The surrounding skin may be normal, pigmented or distorted by an underlying mass.

- These tracts are a potential pathway for infections within the dura mater, the tough outer membrane covering the brain, and may also irritate the skin.
- If the tract expands into the thecal sac (the sac that contains the spinal cord) to form a cyst, the mass may appear as a tethered cord. In these circumstances bladder dysfunction usually occurs.

Treatment for Dermal Sinus:

- Sinuses above the lumbosacral region should be surgically removed.
- Although approximately 25 percent of presumed sacral sinuses seen at birth will regress to a deep dimple on follow-up, all dermal sinuses should be surgically explored and treated prior to development of neurologic symptoms or signs of infection.
- The results of treatment following intradural infection are never as good as when undertaken prior to infection.

- Sinuses that terminate on the tip of the tailbone rarely penetrate the dura and may not need to be treated unless local infection occurs.

CHAPTER 9

THE URINARY TRACT AND KIDNEYS

The urinary tract consists of urethra (the tube connecting the bladder to the outside of the body) the bladder, the kidneys and the ureters (the tube that connect the kidneys to the bladder). Almost all babies with Spina Bifida have normal kidney function. However, the nerves that control the bladder are almost always abnormal due to damage. This is because the nerves did not properly form during conception stage. As a result the bladder will have trouble storing urine as well emptying the bladder may be an issue that causes the urine to drip out constantly.

The bladder functions under very low pressure, and holds a certain capacity. When the bladder is full sensory receptors sends a message from the nerves in the spinal cord to the brain and lets it know the bladder needs emptying. People with Spina Bifida are not able to feel when their bladders are full; this can lead to several problems like urinary tract infections.

A urinary tract infection happens when the bacteria from the area surrounding the urethra (urinary opening) gets into the bladder. If the bacterium stays in the bladder a bladder infection will occur. A bladder infection is not usually associated with a fever, and generally does not produce any long term-damage to the bladder or kidneys. If the bacterium enters the kidneys, it is called a kidney infection or pyelonephritis. If the urine is infected this can cause severe damage to the kidneys.

A kidney infection is usually associated with a high fever and may produce permanent damage or scarring of the kidney even after only one infection. Kidney damage can occur without you knowing it. In addition the high pressure can be reached in the bladder causing the urine to move back towards the kidneys, a condition called vesicoureteral reflux. This condition does not have visible symptoms. This is why many people with Spina Bifida catheterize themselves using a tube to insert in the bladder to drain the urine out.

Urinary tract infections are more common in girls. While it is unusual for boys to develop a urinary tract infection, it does happen occasionally. Many children with Spina Bifida are sometimes required to take a medicine called anticholinergic. This will help with relaxing the bladder so it can store more urine and to protect the kidneys.

Symptoms of UTI:

Babies and toddlers

- Fever
- Strange smelling urine
- Child is not often hungry
- Vomiting
- Child is fussy

Older kids and Adults

- Muscle aches
- Feeling tired, shaky, and weak
- A frequent and intense urge to urinate
- Only small amount of urine passed, despite a strong urge to urine
- Cloudy, red, pink, dark, or bloody urine that has a foul smell
- Pain in lower back or abdominal area of the bladder (generally below the navel)
- Nausea or vomiting
- Fatigue
- Decreased appetite
- A painful burning or stinging sensation during urination

- Loss of bladder control
- Fever/chills (though this is not always present
- Belly feels heavy or tender
- Frequent night waking to go to the bathroom
- Wetting problems, even though the child is toilet taught

How to prevent urinary tract infection (UTI):

- Give plenty of fluids (water is best) every day
- Certain juices, such as cranberry or blueberry
- Wear loose fitting underwear
- Always use a clean catheterization
- Medication
- A toilet timing/training program
- Clean intermittent catheterization
- Making sure child is urinating about every two hours during the day
- Encourage the child not to hold the urine
- Females should wipe front to back after each bathroom uses
- Clear constipation

Chart on Foods, Liquids and Medicines that can harm the bladder:

Food & Drink	Effects on Incontinence	What to Do
Too much water	Overfills the bladder	Drink no more than 2 liters (about 2 quarts) of fluid a day. Drink most of the fluids during the daytime and limit fluid in the evening
Too little fluid	Irritates the bladder. Promotes infection.	Drink at least 1 liter (about 1 quart) of fluid every day.
Alcoholic beverages	Causes dehydration by increasing the amount of urine. Interferes with brain's signals to the bladder about the release urine.	Cut down on or eliminate alcohol.

Drinks and foods containing caffeine (coffee, tea, colas or chocolate)	Stimulates the bladder. Acts as diuretics, producing more urine	Reduce or eliminate caffeine from you diet
Acidic foods and drinks (such as citrus fruits, coffee, tea, and tomatoes)	Irritates the bladder.	Cut down or avoid these items
Carbonated drinks	Irritates sensitive bladders	Use sparingly or not at all
Spicy foods	Irritates the bladder.	Avoid these foods.
Sugar, honey, and Artificial sweeteners	Irritates the bladder.	Limit your use of these foods, if possible.

Medicine	Effects on Incontinence	What to Do
High Blood Pressure Medicine (diuretic, "water pills", channel blockers and others)	Some increase urine output. Some relax the bladder allowing urine to escape	Let your doctor know that your medication may be making incontinence worse. Ask your doctor if you can adjust the dose or switch to another medication to lower your blood pressure. If you cannot switch or adjust medications, ask your doctor about ways to limit the incontinence symptoms.

Antidepressants, Sedatives and Tranquilizers	Some hinder ability of the bladder to contract Some decrease your awareness of the need to urinate	Ask your doctor about switching to another medication or to another type of therapy to treat your depression.
Muscle relaxants	Relaxes bladder muscles.	Use only if necessary. Ask your doctor about steps to limit incontinence side effects.
Sleeping pills	Reduces your awareness that the bladder is full	Explore alternatives to sleeping pills, such as exercising regularly to sleep better, or launching a bedtime ritual.

Tests done to image the bladder, ureters, and kidneys:

- Renal Ultrasound: This test shows the size of the kidneys and weather they are enlarged.
- Voiding cystourethrogram (VCUG): This test looks at the ureters and bladder to make sure that the urine does not get forced up the wrong way, back into the ureter and kidneys during voiding.
- Renal Scan: This test shows how well and how fast the blood filters through the kidney.
- Urodynamic Evaluation: This test measure thee stiffness in the bladder wall.
- Urinalysis: This measures various compounds that passes through the urine
- Cystoscopy: This test is done when a child has vesicoureteral reflux to evaluate the appearance of the urinary tract.
- Creatinine: This blood test shows how well the kidneys are filtering the blood.
- Urinalysis: Also known as a urine "dip" or dipstick test. This test evaluated the kidneys and bladder.

Yes There Is Hope!

Our favorite quote is "Sometimes real super heroes live in the hearts of small children fighting big battles." -Conrad and Erin Bauer

Never tell your child "Don't try, you might get hurt." You never know what your child can do if they don't try. -Patricia Caballero

My favorite quote is by Eleanor Roosevelt, "You gain strength, courage and confidence by every experience in which you really stop to look fear in the face. You must do the thing you think you cannot do." - Carla Schlitt Geiger

Don't give up. I am 61 year old and still walk with long leg braces and crutches. My orthopedic doctor says I should not be able to do this as well as be so independent. I am also married with three grown kids everyone said it could not be done in my case it was possible. -Debbie Dahl Marx

My favorite quote is by Charles Spurgeon, "Anxiety does not empty tomorrow of its sorrows, but only empties today of its strength." This quote reminds me that I don't need to worry I can trust the medical professionals and God to do what is best for my baby. Each baby is a miracle, no matter his or her situation. -Veronica Campbell

There's no question that parenting a child with Spina Bifida is tough and requires doing things you never thought of when you first dreamed of having a child. But the things that at first seem overwhelming become routine and you develop a bond with your child and an appreciation for their strength that is a blessing. -Julleanna Outten Seely

My favorite bible verse is Psalm 139:14 "For thou hast possessed my reins: thou hast covered me in my mother's womb. I will praise thee; for I am fearfully and wonderfully made: marvelous are thy works; and that my soul knoweth right well. My substance was not hid from three, when I was in secret, and curiously wrought in the lowest parts of the earth. Thine eyes did see my substance, yet being unperfect; and in thy book all my members were written, which in continuance were fashioned, when as yet there was none of them." -Christa Bauman

Certa bonum certamen is Latin for fight the good fight. -Brendan Ball

My favorite bible verse is "I can do all things through Christ who strengthen me! (Philippians 4:13) -Cornelius Burr

My favorite bible verse is, "Let everything that has breathe praise the Lord!" (Psalm 150:6) -Natasha M.

CHAPTER 10

HOW SPINA BIFIDA AFFECTS THE BOWEL

The majority of children with Spina Bifida are at risk for constipation and bowel incontinence because the nerves that regulate in the lowest level of the spinal cord do not form properly often causing nerve damage. The nerves that are damaged generally affect three areas of the bowels: the sphincter muscles, the mechanism which tell us that the rectum is full, and the muscles which aid the body in removing fecal waste. This typically does not become an issue until your child begins eating solid foods. However, few children with Spina Bifida have the complete function of the bowels and constipation is quite common, while other children with Spina Bifida require the help of laxative to keep them stooling regularly. Prevention of constipation is essential for eventually attaining stool continence.

Different Components of the bowel:

- **Small Intestine**-The small intestine is a tubular structure within the abdominal cavity that carries the food in continuation with the stomach up to the colon from where the large intestine carries it to the rectum and out of the body through the anus. The main function of this organ is to aid in digestion.

- **Large Intestine-**The large intestine comprises of the second part of the alimentary canal. The large intestine consists of the cecum and colon. It begins at the right iliac region of the pelvis (the region just at or below the right waist) where it continues from the small intestine and continues up the abdomen. Therefore after it traverses across the width of the abdominal cavity, and then it turns down, continuing to its endpoint at the anus.

- **Rectum-**The rectum is the terminal segment of the digestive system in which feces accumulate just prior to discharge.

Types of bowel incontinence:

- Urge incontinence
- Flatus incontinence
- Passive incontinence
- Anal and rectal incontinence
- Overflow incontinence

- Dual incontinence

Causes of incontinence:

- Diarrhea
- Constipation
- Muscle damage or weakness
- Nerve damage
- Loss of stretch in the rectum
- Childbirth by vaginal delivery
- Hemorrhoids and rectal prolapse
- Rectocele
- Inactivity

Sign and symptoms of bowel incontinence:

- The anus is irritated
- Diarrhea
- The anus is itchy
- Constipation
- Bloating
- Abdominal pain
- Abdominal cramping
- Flatulence
- Urinary incontinence

List of bowel management techniques:

- Bowel training and timing- Patients with lack of sphincter control or low awareness of the urge to defecate may find a bowel-training program effective. It includes exercises that restore the strength of vital muscles for bowel control. Bowel training may involve learning to go to the toilet at certain times of the day, such as after a meal. If bowel movements occur at specific times each day it often becomes easier for the patient to regain control.

- Medication and Supplements- Bulk forming laxatives, Stool softeners, Lubricates, Stimulants, Osmotics, Hyperosmotics all used to soften the stool and provide daily emptying of the bowel.

- Enemas and Bowel Washouts- These have to be prescribed by your doctor or continence adviser. They are put inside the bottom as high as possible to help get things moving.

- Stool impaction treatment- if laxative or enema does not solve the stool impaction problem the doctor may have to remove it. With two gloved fingers the physician breaks the stool into small pieces, making them easier to expel.

- Diet- Eat a high-fiber diet, which include lots of fruit, vegetables and cereals. Drink plenty of water this helps to keep the feces soft, so going to the toilet is easier.

- Exercise- helps to keep your bowel fit!

- Operation- There are several operations that can help control your bowels. One current procedure is called the Chait Cecostomy procedure. Contact a continence adviser or your doctor if you want to know more.

- Biofeedback- Involved providing visual feedback rewards for successively stronger sphincter contractions during training sessions and requiring 50 sphincter contraction exercises daily.

- Adaptive clothing- Adaptive clothing makes it easier to dress and be dressed. Adaptive clothes are ideal for disabled, limited mobility or restricted arm and leg movement, and elderly.

Tests done to identify cause of bowel incontinence:

- Stool testing
- Endoscopy
- Anorectal ultrasonography
- Endosonography
- Nerve tests
- MRI defecography
- Anal manometry
- Defecography
- Anal electromyography (EMG)
- Flexible sigmoidoscopy or colonoscopy

Treatment for incontinence:

- Eating, diet, and nutrition
- Medications
- Bowel training
- Pelvic floor exercises and biofeedback
- Surgery
- Electrical stimulation

Foods with good sources of Fiber:

Nuts and seeds
Almond butter
Almond paste
Almonds
Anise seed
Brazil nuts

Cashew butter
Cashews
Chestnuts
Filberts or hazelnuts
Hickory nuts
Macadamia nuts
Mixed nuts with peanut butter
Mixed nuts without peanut butter
Peanuts
Pecans
Pine nuts-Pignolias
Pine nuts-pinyon
Pistachio nuts
Poppy seeds
Pumpkin seeds
Squash seeds
Quinoa, cooked
Quinoa, dry
Sesame seeds
Sunflower butter
Sunflower seeds

Grains
Amaranth
Barley
Bran muffins
Brown rice
Buckwheat
Bulgur wheat
Corn
Corn bread
Crackers
Granola
Kamut khorasan wheat

Millet
Oats
Oatmeal
Pastas
Quinoa
Rolls
Rye
Sorghum
Spelt Wheat
Triticale
Wheat
Whole grain breads
Wild rice

Vegetables
Beans
Broccoli
Brussels sprouts
Cabbage
Cauliflower
Carrots
Chick Peas
Corn
Eggplant
Garbanzo beans
Greens- Collards, kale, turnips
Lima beans
Mushrooms
Potato with skin
Pumpkin, canned
Peas- black-eyed peas, green peas
Peppers
Rhubarb
Spinach

Squash
Sweet Potatoes

Fruits
Apples
Berries- Blue berries, Blackberries, Raspberries, etc.
Cherries
Dried fruits- Figs, Raisins, Apricots, Dates, etc.
Grapes
Guava
Melons
Orange
Peaches
Pears
Pineapples
Plums
Prunes
Strawberries

Yes There Is Hope!

Always believe in your dreams and anything can happen. -Richard Colman AM

No matter what life gives you always remember that even though the sky may be grey at some point in your life on the other side of them clouds is a big ball of sunshine. -Living with Spina/Myelomeningocele

My son, Christian who has Spina Bifida was asked to speak to his high school his senior year. I remember with clarity one thing that he said, "Don't let anyone tell you that you can't do something! Follow your dreams or they will slip away." It blew me away! It was so profound coming from someone with limited abilities, 18 years old and given a dim future at birth. He has always had a passion for lighting that you would see at a performance or concert. This past Easter he designed and ran the light for worship service featuring double Grammy award winner, Matt Redmen, with over 8,000 people in attendance at our local coliseum. Whatever you do, work at it with all your heart, as working for the Lord, not for human masters. (Colossians 3:23) -Laura Reites

My favorite bible verse is, "With God all things are Possible." (Matthew 19:26) -Megan Cain

I am more than my disability. My disability has helped to shape who I am but I am who I am despite my disability. -Kim Burdick

Never under estimate a child with Spina Bifida. Don't ever give up. -Rea Strother

My favorite quote is from an unknown author, "Live life to the fullest. I have Spina Bifida but Spina Bifida does not have me." -Garth Wheeler

My favorite quote is from Rutherford B. Hayes, "The expert in anything was once a beginner." -Colleen Margaret

Nothing is too big to accomplish, even with a disability. -Rick O'Steen

My favorite bible verse is Philippians 4:13, I can do all things through Christ who strengthens me!" this scripture really gets me through every day of my life when dealing with issues. -Anna Guidry

Chapter 11

What is a Chait Cecostomy Catheter

A Cecostomy procedure is a procedure in which your physician creates an open tract, called a Cecostomy, from the abdominal wall to the intestines for the purpose of providing enemas or other treatment. A short-term standard profile catheter is often placed into the tract for a period of time. After about six weeks the physician will check to see if the track is healed and ensure that no infection is present. If the condition of the tract and surrounding area is appropriate they will remove the short-term catheter and replace it with a long-term low profile Chait catheter. This is an outpatient procedure that is typically 10-15 minutes, if there are no complications. The Chait catheter insertion is easier and quicker than the short-term catheter insertion procedure, and an overnight stay at the hospital may not be necessary.

Once placed, the Chait remains in the cecum and provides a comfortable, convenient way to cleanse the bowels with an enema routine. The enema is given through the Chait and exits the body through the anal opening along the bowel contents. Emptying the colon in this regular, predictable way gives individuals more control over their bowels and helps prevent unexpected soiling, allowing one to become more independent, socially active and secure.

Benefits:

- More socially accepted
- Children can participate in normal activities, including swimming, schooling and family outing.
- Improved self-esteem
- More appealing
- Decreased family stress
- Wheelchair compatible
- Children can become more involved and more independent in performing the bowel cleansing at an earlier age.
- The Chait tube takes pressure away from the bladder, preventing bladder accidents and infections.
- Flushing the coon is less invasive than when using rectal enemas.
- The chait is more comfortable.
- It allows increased mobility.

Complications:

- Discomfort around the tube site.
- Mucous discharge
- Channel may become too narrow as child grows.
- Kink in the appendix
- Minor skin irritation
- Infection around the tube or within the abdomen.
- Stoma stenosis
- Fever and nausea
- Dislodgement of the chait catheter.

Care that is needed at home after surgery:

- Care of the incision: There is an indwelling tube in place with sutures into the appendicocecostomy. Care must be taken to keep this tube in place and secure with tegaderm and tape. Keep it dry. Remove it according to the surgeon's instructions.

- Activity limitations: Quiet supervised play for 24-48 hours. No running, contact sports or vigorous activity for 4 weeks.
- Diet: Your child may have his/her usual diet. Some children become constipated after surgery. Give plenty of fluids to

prevent this. Your child should not go more than 48 hours without a bowel movement.

- Bathing: Sponge bathe/shower your child until the tube is removed.
- Medication: Give pain medicine around the clock for the first 24 hours and as needed after for three to four days. Please call if your child is uncomfortable. Some children require more medicine than other.

When to call the surgery team:

- Fever is greater than 101
- Accidental catheter dislodgement or inability to pass the catheter.
- Nausea or Vomiting
- A crack in the hinge, tube or cap
- Inability to flush the tube
- Infection around the tube or abdomen
- Excessive drainage from around the tube
- A loose, leaky fit between the connecting tube and the cecostomy tube.
- Abdominal distension
- Granulation tissue (Buildup of harmless red tissue around the tube entrance)
- Unusual drainage
- Skin irritation or redness
- Discomfort or skin break down around the tube site

Maintaining the cecostomy tube:

- Clean around the tube everyday with soap and water. Dry the area around and under the tube wall.
- Apply a split 2x2 gauze, if desired. There may be some drainage.
- Change the gauze at least twice a day or more if it becomes soiled or moist. Once the site heals, you do not have to use gauze. Keep the area clean and dry.

When to replace the tube:

- You should replace your child's cecostomy once a year, unless there is a problem. This procedure is done at the hospital in medical imaging (x-ray department). It does not take long to do this and your child does not have to be admitted into the hospital afterwards.

Your child may return to school or daycare:

- Immediately after surgery, your child should not participate in contact sports, while an 'indwelling tube' is in the Malone stoma or while the chait button site is healing. After 2-4 weeks, your child can fully participate in any activities.

Yes There Is Hope

"Life is like a wrestling match it will knock you down but you gotta get back up and fight like a champ". -Quade Louie

My favorite quote is by William Arthur Ward, "If you can imagine it, you can achieve it; if you can dream it, you can become it." - Kayleigh Nichole Offenberger

Don't let people tell you that you can't do something; having Spina Bifida does not stop you. -Sharon Pocock

You are only limited by the limitations in the minds of others. -Doug Anderson

Focus on the things you can do not the things you cannot. -The Wheeling Dragon

When life hands you lemons, make lemonade. -Brandon Buck

Many scars, one story. -Mike Mutz

I am 35 years old with Spina Bifida and hydrocephalus; I was married in 2010 and blessed with a son in 2011. -S.L.T

Favorite saying: No pain, no gain. Favorite bible verse: I can do all thins through Christ who strengths me. (Philippians 4:13) -Casey Followay

My favorite bible verse is "For God so loved the world, that he gave his only begotten Son, that whosoever believeth in him should not perish, but have everlasting life." (John 3:16) - Aaron Sullivan

CHAPTER 12

ORTHOPEDIC AND DEFORMITIES ISSUES

Many infants with Spina Bifida have deformities and orthopedic problems such as clubfeet, hip deformities such as contracture, subluxation, or dislocation. Patients may also have problems with spinal curvatures known as scoliosis, kyphosis, or lordosis. Contractures (tightness) of the knees, hip, and/or ankles may also occur. Both congenital and acquired orthopedic deformities are seen in patients with Spina Bifida. Orthopedic problems may also be caused by iatrogenic injury such as postoperative tethered cord. Babies and children with Spina Bifida are very susceptible to breaking their bones since their bones may be weaker than normal.

Most children with Spina Bifida use wheelchairs due to partial or complete paralysis in their legs. Spinal curvature can cause sitting imbalances that put too much pressure on certain areas causing skin problems and pressure sores. Many spinal deformities in children with Spina Bifida will worsen over time. Along with physical therapist, your orthopedist will decide what kind of surgery, equipment or braces your child may require as he or she grows.

The three most common types of spinal deformity are:

- **Scoliosis**- (sideways curvature of the spine to the left or right). Scoliosis in children with myelomeningocele often results from lack of neuromuscular control not being able to consciously control movement.
- **Kyphosis**- (exaggerated round back). Kyphosis can develop from muscle imbalanced in a child's trunk are associated with paralysis.
- **Lordosis**- (exaggerated sway back). Lordosis can occur when a child's hip muscles are tight causing the pelvis to push forward and exaggerated swayback to develop.

Orthopedics deformities:

- **Congenital deformities** are present at birth and they include clubfoot and vertical talus.
- **Acquired developmental deformities** are related to the level of involvement and are caused by muscle imbalance, paralysis,

and decreased sensation in the lower extremities.

- **Clubfoot**-Is a congenital condition in which the feet are turned in an inward or outward position.
- **Equinus**-A condition that limits the bending motion in the ankle joint and causes tiptoe walking on one or both feet. It is usually associated with clubfoot.
- **Vertical talus**-A rare deformity of the foot, consisting of an irreducible dorsal dislocation of the navicular on the talus producing a rigid rocker-bottom flatfoot.
- **Calcaneus/calcaneovalgus**-Is a congenital deformity that is a combination of the talipes calcaneus and talipes valgus, marked by a dorsifexed, everted, and abducted foot.
- **Ankle valgus**-A condition where the ankles roll in, compromising stability and alignment of the body and may other possible origins.
- **Hindfoot valgus**-Is a specific form of clubfoot, comprising the region of the talus and calcaneus.
- **Cavus/varus/cavovarus**-Cavus is a condition in which the foot has an abnormal arch. Varus is an inward angulation of the distal segment of a bone

or joint. Cavovarus is a foot deformity where the foot arch is very high and the heel slants inward.

- **Skin breakdown/amputation**-Skin breakdown is changes to the intact skin due to minor scrapes, cuts, tears, blisters, or burns to most serious pressure ulcers with the destruction of tissue even including the bone. Amputation is the surgical removal of all or part of a limb or extremity such as an arm, leg, foot, hand, toe or finger.

Orthopedic Imaging tests:

- X-ray
- Degree of curve
- MRI scans

Spina Bifida Level	Prognosis for walking
S2-S4	Frequently walk without aides (braces or crutches) may need shoe inserts.
L5-S1	Usually need short leg braces to help with foot position and push off. May need crutches or crane
L-4	Usually need braces. May be above or below knee. May also use crutches or cane. Some use wheelchairs at older ages.

Yes There Is Hope

My favorite bible verses are, "Do not fear for I am with you; be not dismayed; for I am thy God: I will strengthen thee; yea, I will help thee; yea, I will uphold thee with the right hand of my righteousness. (Isaiah 41:10) For I know the plans I have for you saith the Lord, thoughts of peace, and not of evil, to give you an expected end. (Jeremiah 29:11)" -Autumn Trussell

My favorite quote is by John Michael Montgomery, "Life's a dance sometimes you lead sometimes you follow, life's a dance you learn as you go." -Adam Rayborn

Nothing is easy to the unwilling. -Megan Stapley

My favorite bible verse is, "Be of good courage, and he shall strengthen your heart, all ye that hope in the Lord." (Psalms 31:24) -Peter McNeal

My favorite encouraging statement is found in the Doctrine and Covenants, "And if you keep my commandments, and endure to the end, you shall have eternal life, which gift is the greatest of all gifts of God." (Doctrine and Covenants 14:7) -Kanda Bain Fernelius

My favorite bible verse is "For I know the plans I have for you," declares the Lord, "plans to prosper you and not harm you, to give hope and future." (Jeremiah 29:11) -Margaret A. Clark

I always told my daughter you can do anything anyone else does you just have to do it differently. -Brenda Pennington Womack

I have always taught my daughter that "it's not a big deal" cause in all reality it isn't. I also use everything happens for a reason. -Jessica Westman

My favorite bible verse is Philippians 4:13, I can do all things through Christ who strengthens me. -Deevora Jones

When I found out that our daughter had Spina Bifida, I was 16 weeks pregnant. We were terrified, but we knew that God had a plan. I clung to Isaiah 41:10, "Fear thou not; for I am with thee: be not dismayed; for I am thy God: I will strengthen thee; yea, I will help thee; yea I will uphold thee with the right hand of my righteousness."

We knew that God would provide for the needs as long as we were faithful in following Him. He gives us strength each day. Our daughter is such a blessing that worlds cannot even begin to describe the depths of joy God has given us through her life. She is almost 8. It hasn't been easy, but with every challenge, comes victory. We now live a life full of victories. - Jennifer King Camp

CHAPTER 13

OTHER RELATED MEDICAL ISSUES

Spina Bifida Health care Programs:

The Spina Bifida health care program covers most services and supplies that are medically or psychologically necessary. The Department of Veterans Affairs administers this program. Vietnam and certain Koreans Veterans who have birth children born with Spina Bifida (except for Spina Bifida occulta) are eligible for a monthly monetary allowance. The program provides reimbursement for travel to and from the doctor, medical services, supplies and health care facility.

Effective October 10, 2008, changes were made to Public Law 110-387, Section 408 this outlines the benefits available under the Spina Bifida program. As a result, medical services and supplies for Spina Bifida beneficiaries are no longer limited. Some services require specific advance approval or preauthorization. Eligibility determinations must be first made through the Denver VA Regional Office.

The VA will determine the current level of disability upon receipt of both medical lay evidence and completed Application for Spina Bifida Benefits (VA FORM). Once eligibility is determined Spina Bifida awardees (or guardians) are automatically contacted and registered for health care benefits.

Program Requirements:

Your birth father or mother must have:

- Served in Vietnam during the period from January 9, 1962, through May 7, 1975
- Served in or near the Korean Demilitarized Zone (DMZ) during the period from April 1, 1968, through August 31, 1971, and have been exposed to herbicides.

Preauthorization is required for the following:

- Attendants
- Dental services
- Dural medical equipment (in excess of $2,000)
- Mental health services
- Organ transplants
- Substance abuse treatment
- Training of family members

- Travel (other than mileage for travel)
- Hospice care
- Transplantation services

To request preauthorization, include the following:

- Beneficiary's name
- Beneficiary's Social Security Number (SSN)
- Description of service requested to include procedure and diagnosis codes
- Estimated cost (if know)
- Medical justification for services requested
- Name, Address, and Telephone number of the provider who will actually furnish the requested services
- The anticipated date of service
- Veteran's name
- Veteran's Social Security Number (SSN)

Yes There Is Hope

God only gives you as much as you can handle. -Brandy Jamrock

My favorite bible verse is "For God so love the world that he gave his only begotten Son, that whosoever believeth in him should not perish, but have everlasting life." (John 3:16) -Erica Reddick

"I can do all things through him who give me strength."(Philippians 4:13)   Never consider yourself to have a disability, because in disability there is the word ability -Katie Soileau Fonteno

If God brings you to it, he will bring you through it. -Sharanda Nicodemus

My favorite quote by Push Girls is, "If you can't stand up stand out there gonna stare there gonna talk give them a reason and be yourself always." -Jessica Snyder

My favorite bible verse is, "God is within her, she will not fall; God will help her at break of the day. (Psalm 46:5) -Rebecca Guzel

This sickness is not unto death but for the glory of God. -Yvonne Milton

For thou hast possessed my reins: thou hast covered me in my mother's womb. I will praise three; for I am fearfully and wonderfully made: marvellous are thy works; and that my soul knoweth right well. My substance was not hid from thee, when I was made in secret, and curiously wrought in the lowest parts of the earth. Thine eyes did see my substance, yet being unperfect; and in thy book all my members were written, which in continuance were fashioned, when as yet there was none of them. (Psalm 139:13-16) -Wendy Wieland

Don't let anyone tell you what you can and can't do, and if you're a parent to a child with Spina Bifida don't treat them like they are made of glass. -Chris Behrens

We learn from our mistakes, as long as we don't repeat them, if we want to succeed in anything we do, we have to try and not to be discouraged by failures. If we never fail it means we never tried. -Judith Smith

CHAPTER 14

HEALTH CHECK

Every person needs a primary health care provider, e.g., a pediatrician, family doctor, or nurse practitioner. The primary care provider will want to make sure that your child is healthy; developing normally; and receiving immunization against diseases and infections, including the flu.

In addition to seeing a primary health care provider, a person with Spina Bifida will be checked and treated as needed by doctors who specialize in different parts of the body. These doctors might suggest treatment or surgeries to help the person.

These specialists might include:

- An orthopedist, who will work with muscles and bones.
- An urologist, who will check the kidneys and bladder.
- Neurosurgeon, who will check the brain and spine.

Other concerns

- Learning
- Relating to others
- Vision
- Staying at a healthy weight
- Depression

Yes There Is Hope

My favorite quote is by Sandra Kring, "The tiny seed knew that in order to grow, it needed to be dropped in dirt, covered in darkness, struggle to reach the light." -D.S.

A challenge is just an opportunity to make you better. -Amanda Gault

If God got you to it, He'll get you through it. -Nicole M. Small

My favorite bible verse is, "Have I not commanded you? Be strong and courageous. Do not be afraid; do not be discouraged, for the Lord your God will be with you wherever you go."(Joshua 1:9) -Danielle Moore's favorite bible verse

My favorite quote is by Lucille Ball, "I'd rather regret the things I've done than regret the things I haven't done. The more things you do, the more you can do." -D.K.

My favorite quote is by Wayne Gretzky, "You miss 100% of the shots you don't take!" -Katie Firefly

My favorite bible verse is, "For I know the plans I have for you," declares the Lord, "Plans to prosper you and not to harm you, plans to give you hope and a future. (Jeremiah 29:11) -Janice Craven

My favorite bible verse is, "And we know that in all things God works for the good of those who love him. Who have been called according to his purpose" (Romans 8:28) -Geoffery Liegel

My favorite bible verse is, "Therefore, since we have been justified through faith, we have peace with God through our Lord Jesus Christ through whom we have gained access by faith into the grace in which we now stand. And we boast in the hope of the glory of God. Not only so, but also glory in our sufferings, because we know that suffering produces perseverance; perseverance, Character; and character, hope. And hope does not put us to shame, because God's love has been poured out into our hearts through the Holy Spirit, who has been given to us. (Romans 5:1-5) -Sarie Leavitt Wambaja

My favorite quote is a Japanese Proverb, "Fall seven times, stand up eight."-Susan Umback

CHAPTER 15

OBESITY

Obesity is a complex disorder involving an excessive amount of body fat. It is the most common nutritional issue in North America. Obesity is not the same as being overweight, which means weighing too much. Obesity is determined by ones (BMI) Body Mass Index or by using calipers to measure the skin-folds and jotting down the results on a standardized chart. In 2012, more than 40 million children under the age of 5 were overweight or obese.

It is reported that in America 50% of children with Spina Bifida, especially those with hydrocephalus are at greater risk for obesity. Obesity has unwanted effects on the cardiovascular system that can limit mobility which causes less activity, less lean body mass, lower metabolic rate making it harder for the individual to keep up with their peers in social and work situations. At least 30 minutes of regular, moderate-intensity physical activity reduce the risk of cardiovascular disease, diabetes, colon cancer and breast cancer.

Muscle strengthening and balance training can reduce falls and improve mobility among older children and adults. More activity may be required for weight control. Extra weight can create major health problems such as heaviness on the skin causing pressure sore or skin break down for those in wheelchairs or using orthotics. The potential for bone fractures is also a threat.

Health effects:

- Obese children are more likely to have risk factors for cardiovascular disease, such as high cholesterol (blocks the arteries and blood cannot move through) or high levels of triglycerides and LDL ("bad") cholesterol and low levels of HDL ("good") cholesterol. In a population-based sample of 5-17 years olds 70% of obese youth had at least one risk factor for cardiovascular disease.

- Obese adolescents are more likely to have pre-diabetes, a condition in which blood glucose levels indicates a high risk for development of diabetes.

- Children and adolescents who are obese are at greater risk for bone and joint problems such as stigmatization and poor self-esteem.

Long-term health effects:

- Children and adolescents who are obese are likely to be obese as adults and are therefore more at risk for adult health problems such as heart disease, Type II diabetes (body cannot take in insulin and is prevented from generating enough energy), stroke, several types cancer, and osteoarthritis. One study showed that children, who became obese as early as age 2, were more likely to be obese as adults.

- Overweight and obesity are associated with increased risk for many types of cancers, including cancer of the breast, colon, endometrium, esophagus, kidney, pancreas, gall bladder, liver, thyroid, ovary, cervix, and prostate, as well as multiple myeloma and Hodgkin's lymphoma.

Prevent obesity:

- Healthy lifestyle habits, including healthy eating and physical activity, can lower the risk of becoming obese and developing related diseases.

- Increase consumption of fruits, vegetables, legumes, whole grains and nuts.

- Limit the intake of total fats, sugars, and salt.

- The dietary and physical activity behaviors of children and adolescents are influenced by many sectors of society, including families, communities, schools, child care settings, medical care providers, faith-based institutions, government agencies, the media and the food and beverage industries and entertainment industries.

- Schools play a particularly critical role by establishing a safe and supportive environment with policies and practices that support healthy behaviors. Schools also provide opportunities for students to learn about and practice healthy eating and physical activity behaviors.

Yes There Is Hope

My favorite bible verse is, "The wages of sin is death but the gift of God is eternal Life through Christ Jesus our Lord." (Romans 6:23) While my favorite quote is, "To dream of the person you want to be is a waste of the person you are. - Christle Brown Chizzle Chapman

My favorite bible verse is, "I will praise you because I am fearfully and wonderfully made; your works are wonderful, I know that full well." (Psalm 139:14) While my favorite quote is what Les Brown said, "Shoot for the moon. Even if you miss, you'll land among the stars." -Heath Sandy Hall

"Your walk talks, and your talk talks, but your walk talks louder than your talk talks. - Anna Mccain-King

My favorite bible verse is, "For God has not given us a spirit of fear and timidity, but of power, love, and self- discipline." (2 Timothy 1:7) -Erica Lambert Bowen

My favorite bible verse is, "For God so loved the world that he gave his one and only Son, that whoever believes in him shall not perish but have eternal life." (John 3:16) -Bruce Legacie

My favorite bible verse is, "Nothing is impossible for God." (Luke 1:37) -A.O.C

"This too shall pass." -Anita Jimenez

My favorite bible verse is I can do all things through Christ who strengthens me. (Philippians 4:13) -Carol Daniel Hammans

Giving up is not an option! -A. Scott

The prayer I often go back to and find most relevant to my condition is the serenity prayer. God, grant me the serenity to accept the things I cannot change, the courage to change the things I can, and the wisdom to know the difference. We can have ops and physio and do things to make ourselves as functional as possible, but we also need to accept that we have limitations. Finding the balance between pushing yourself to achieve and being too hard on yourself is sometimes the greatest challenge of all. -Gill Raine

CHAPTER 16

DEPRESSION AND ANXIETY

Depression and anxiety are two mental health concerns that plague our society greatly. Depression and anxiety are different conditions, but are often intertwined. Both depression and anxiety treatments are similar, which explains why the two disorders are often confused. At any point in time, 3 to 5 percent of people suffer from major depression the lifetime risk is about 17 percent. In people with Spina Bifida and shunted hydrocephalus, this is especially important because many signs and symptoms of depression may actually be caused by medical conditions (shunt malfunction, infections, or medications). In those situations, the symptoms disappear when the underlying medical conditions is treated or corrected.

When depression and anxiety interfere with your life it can cause pain for you and those who care about you. Depression and anxiety are common but is a serious illness. Those suffering from depression and anxiety can seek a professional who can offer valuable support.

If you are suffering from depression and anxiety:

The best way to treat depression or anxiety is to become as informed as possible about treatment options, which can help you re-learn your ability to cope with stress. Both conditions usually improve with psychological counseling and medications, such as antidepressant. A psychiatrist is the best health care professional to see for providing care for people with mental health problems. The sooner you start your treatments, the sooner you can recover.

Symptoms of depression:

- Early morning waking/or excessive sleepiness
- Sleeping disorders (too much or too little)
- Losing or gaining weight
- Loss of Appetite/overeating
- Low mood with or without diurnal variation
- Anxiety and Irritability
- Social withdrawal
- Loss of sex drive or and/sexual problems
- Loss of self-confidence and self-esteem
- Self-blame and inappropriate guilt
- Inability to make decisions

- Difficulty concentrating
- Slowed down thinking
- Loss of functional or self-care skills
- Thinking about suicide and death
- Depressive delusion
- Aggression
- Irritability

Symptoms of Anxiety:

- Feeling of panic, fear, and uneasiness
- Problems sleeping
- Cold or sweaty hand and/or feet
- Shortness of breath
- Heart Palpitations
- An inability to be still or calm
- Dry mouth
- Numbness or tingling in the hands or feet
- Nausea
- Muscles tension
- Dizziness

Treatment for depression and Anxiety:

- Give medication time to work
- Put effort into therapy
- Make some lifetime changes
- Get a second opinion

- Focus on small steps
- Be an active partner in your treatment

Yes There Is Hope

My favorite bible verse is, 'for I know the plans I have for you, "declares the LORD." Plans to proper you and not to harm you, plans to give you hope and a future.' -Rebecca Landreth

Take it one day at a time. Read books about Spina Bifida but ultimately read your child they may not always be textbook. -Toni Roohr

My favorite bible verse is, 'for I am not ashamed of gospel, because it is the power of God that brings salvation to everyone who believes: first to the Jew, then to the Gentile.' (Romans 1:6) -Dereck D Cooper

My favorite bible verse is, 'the Lord is my light and my salvation; whom shall I fear? The Lord is the strength of my life; of whom shall I be afraid. (Psalms 27:1) -Ebony Bray

My favorite quote is by singer Bob Marley, 'you will never know how strong you are until being strong is the only choice you have.' -Hope Wooldridge

"Scott Hamilton said, the only disability in life is a bad attitude. -Janae Packman

My favorite quote is by Neil Marcus, "Disability is not a 'brave Struggle' or 'courage in the face of adversity'...disability is an art. It's an ingenious way to live. -Jesus Arroyo

Faith makes things possible not easy. After shunt replacement I was crying in my daughters neurosurgeons arms and she said, "The solution is the next, but if we give up we will never know." -Jennifer Lynn Albitre

"Captain Jack Sparrow said, the problem is not the problem; the problem is your attitude about the problem." -Mikie Sampson

Control what you can, and let go of the rest. - H.C.M

CHAPTER 17

AGENT ORANGE BENEFITS ACT

The U.S military sprayed approximately 20 million gallons of Agent Orange a highly toxic herbicide on trees and vegetation during the Vietnam War between 1962 and 1971 to remove unwanted plant life and leaves which provided cover for the enemy forces. Several decades later, concerns about the health effect from these chemicals continue. Some research efforts have suggested that there may be relationship between exposure by the Vietnam veterans to Agent Orange/herbicides and the subsequent development of Spina Bifida in some of their children.

In 1996 President Clinton signed into law the Agent Orange Benefits Act, Public Law 102-204. This law is a benefits package for Vietnam veterans whose children were born with Spina Bifida. The Agent Orange Benefits Act authorized the Department of Veterans Affairs to provide certain benefits effective October 1, 1997. The Department of Veterans Affairs has developed a comprehensive program to respond to these medical problems and concerns. The VA offers eligible Veterans a free Agent Orange Registry health exam for possible long-term health problems related to exposure.

If you want to qualify for VA disability benefits for dioxin exposure in or outside of Vietnam or Korea, you should be able to show three things.

- Proof of service in Vietnam from January 9, 1962 and May 7, 1975, this includes brief visits ashore or service aboard a ship that operated on the inland waterways of Vietnam.

- In or near the Korean demilitarized zone anytime between September 1967 and August 1971.

- Evidence that your illness began within the time the VA has specified for your particular disease.

Veterans who meet the three criteria do not have to prove they were exposed to Agent Orange; the VA presumes that Agent Orange caused their illness. If you do not meet the three criteria, you may qualify under the Blue Water veterans-Service members aboard U.S. Navy and Coast Guard ships off the coast of Vietnam may have been exposed. Children of Vietnam era who suffer from birth defects such as Spina Bifida can also qualify for benefits.

Agent Orange Symptoms and Effects:

The most distinguishing effects of dioxin poisoning are:

- Chloracne
- Liver dysfunction
- Severe personality disorders
- Cancers
- Birth defects

Symptoms and Effects:

<u>Gastrointestinal:</u>

- Loss of appetite (Anorexia)
- Nausea
- Vomiting
- Diarrhea
- Constipation
- Yellowing of eyes, skin, and urine (Jaundice)
- Liver Inflammation (Hepatitis)
- Abdominal pain
- Gastric hyperplasia
- Gastric ulcers

Genitourinary:

- Stones
- Burning
- Bloody urine (Hermaturia)
- Dribbling
- Brown urine
- Bladder discomfort
- Kidney pain

Neurological:

- Tingling
- Numbness
- Dizziness
- Headaches
- Twitching, Fidgeting, etc. (Automatic dyscontrol)
- Suspension of breath (sleep apnea)
- Incoordination
- Unnaturally
- Drowsy (Hypersomnolence)
- Loss of sensation in extremities

Psychiatric:

- Violent
- Irritable
- Angry
- Severe depression

- Suicide
- Frenzied (Manic)
- Tremulous
- Memory loss
- Loss of concentration
- Severe personality changes

Metabolic:

- Fatigue
- Rapid weight loss
- Spontaneous fever
- Chills

Cardiovascular:

- Elevated blood pressure
- Blood deficiency

Skin:

- Chloracne
- Rash
- Increased sensitivity (heat)
- Increased sensitivity (sun)
- Altered skin color
- Loss of hair
- Brittle nails

Cancer:

- Tumors
- Liver
- Lung
- Testicular
- Ear duct

Family:

- Miscarriages, child's death, Birth defects
- Cleft Palates
- Open eye
- Kidney abnormalities
- Enlarged liver
- Enlarged head
- Club foot
- Intestinal hemmorage
- Missing or abnormal fingers, toes
- Missing, abnormal, or displaced body parts

Endocrine:

- Enlarged male mammary glands (Gynecomastia)
- Excessive milk flow nipples (Galactorrhea)
- Decreased sexual drive
- Difficulty maintaining and erection

Vision/hearing:

- Blurring
- Burning
- Hearing loss

Respiratory:

- Difficulty or painful breath (Dyspenea)
- Shortness of breath

How to Apply:

- Apply online using e-Benefits, OR
- Work with an accredited representative or agent, OR
- Go to a VA regional office and have a VA employee assist you.

Yes There Is Hope

My favorite quote is by Author J. M. Barrie, "To live would be an awful big adventure." -Kate Stefansson

My favorite bible verse is, "Whom the Lord set free is free indeed." (John 8:36) -Andrea Cooper

I am not ashamed of Jesus. -Sami Brewer Greenhaw

Henry Ford said it best, "Whether you think you can or you think you can't, you're right." - B.W.B

My favorite quote is by Yoda from the movie Empire Strikes Back, "Do, or do not. There is not try," -Keiran Raine

My favorite bible verse, "For I know the thoughts that I think towards you, saith the LORD, thoughts of peace, and not evil, to give you an expected end." (Jeremiah 29:11) -Jennifer Gilmer Djordjevic

My favorite quote is from Elizabeth Kuber-Ross, 'People are like stain glass windows. They sparkle and shine when the sun is out, but when the darkness sets in their true beauty is revealed only if there is light from within. -Jeanie Jones Marsden

There's not enough darkness in all the universe, to sniff the light out of one little candle. -Kinney Leonard

If the grass is greener on the other side, water your own. -Terra Harmon's favorite quote

Look at the physical and see what's inside. There lays the truth. -Author Patrick Williams

CHAPTER 18

LIPOMYELOMENINGOCELE AND LIPOMA

What is spinal cord lipomyelomeningocele?

Lipomyelomeningocele is a lesion that is associated with Spina Bifida and becomes evident within the first few months to years of life. It is classified as an occult lesion. As a result many people who have lipomyelomeningocele may not know they have it. This condition affects females more than males, in a 1.5 to 1 ratio. This condition is abnormal fat accumulation that starts below the level of the skin and extends from the spinal cord into the tissue of the back. Surgery is typically done when the infant is several months of age to repair this issue. The lesion is covered with skin and fat and is not painful.

Lipomyelomeningocele is found in the lower spine area known as the lumbosacral region. Over 90% of patients have soft tissue swelling over the spine in the lumbosacral region. Most infants born with lipomyelomeningocele will not have hydrocephalus water on the brain. One out of three patients may have problems with their legs, while other patients may have bladder and bowel difficulties. Some children will need additional surgery as they grow due to tethered spinal cord.

Symptoms of Lipomyelomeningocele:

- Weakness
- Changes in the color of the skin
- Hairy patches or masses
- Pain
- Limitation of back mobility
- Soft tissue swelling
- Lose neurological function
- Bladder and Bowel incontinence

Potential Investigation for Lipomyelomeningocele:

- Magnetic Resonance Imaging (MRI)
- Spinal Ultrasonography
- Plain Radiography
- Urodynamic Studies
- Serial Somatosensory-Evoked Potential observation
- Computed Tomography (CT) Myelography
- Ultrasound of the spine
- X-Ray

- Renal ultrasound

Lipomyelomeningocele treatment:

- Surgical treatment is recommended when the patient reaches two months or at the time of diagnosis if symptoms occur at a later age.
- The goal of the surgery is to release the attachment of the fat (tethering) to the spinal cord and reduce the bulk of the fatty tumor.
- Watch and wait Performing surgery when symptoms dictate.

Surgery:

- Preserving spinal cord tissue
- Untethering the cord
- Debulking the fatty mass
- Re-establishing normal anatomy in the region

Yes There Is Hope

My favorite bible verse is, 'For I am not ashamed of the gospel, for it is the power of God and the salvation for all who believes in it.' (Romans 1:16) -Tom Beards Jr.

"Man fears most of that evil which lurks in his own heart. -Author B Morgan

My favorite quote is by Albert Pine, 'what we do for ourselves dies with us. What we do for others and the world remains and is immortal.' - S. Casey

Never be ashamed of your scars, they are proof that you are stronger than whatever tried to hurt you. -Jennifer Morgan

Only when you embrace your limitations can you master your capabilities. -John Craig

Why worry when you can pray? -Carissa Delgado's favorite saying by her grandmother Katie "MaeDean" Winters

Famous hockey player Wayne Gretzky, said, 'You miss all the shots you don't take.' -Charlene Childers

My favorite bible verse is, 'I am the vine, you are the branches'. (John 15:5) -Tina Fitzgerald

My favorite bible verse is, 'I can do all things through Christ who strengthens me.' (Philippians 4:13) -Keri Womack

Vivian Greene said, 'It's not waiting for the storms to pass, it's about learning how to dance in the rain.' -Sandee Faasse Russo

CHAPTER 19

WHAT IS SPINAL CORD LIPOMA?

Spinal cord lipoma is associated with a fatty mass or tumor in or around the spinal cord. About 1 in 1,000 people develop this. They may be symptomatic and appear most often in adults, ages 40 to 60 years of age, but can also be found in younger adults and children. Spinal cord lipomas not associated with Spina Bifida are rare lesions that affect both males and females equally, although solitary lipomas are more common in women and multiple lipomas occur more frequently in men. There are many different types of lipomas. They vary in size from pea-sized to the size of an egg or even larger in diameter.

The cause of lipomas is unknown. Your risk of developing this type of skin lump increases if you have a family history of lipomas. Lipomas can be described as a rubbery bulge usually moveable, and are generally painless. Rarely, a lipoma may press a nerve and causes pain or problems. One or more lipomas may be present at the same time. A lipoma is classified as benign growths (tumors) of fatty tissue this means that it is not cancerous and do not metastasize (spread to other organs) and is usually harmless.

A minor injury such as blunt blow to the area can trigger the growth. Being over- weight does not cause lipomas. If they become painful or if you are self-conscious about yours, you can always have it removed surgically.

Sign and Symptoms of Lipomas:

- Dome-shaped or egg shaped lump
- Roundish masses
- Feels soft or rubbery to the touch (easily moveable under the skin with fingers)
- Situated just under the skin
- Pale or colorless
- Generally small
- Sometimes painful
- Remain the same size for years or grow slowly
- Numbness
- Tingling
- Weakness
- Stiffness of the extremities
- Urinating or Bowel movement incontinence

Types of Lipomas:

- **Conventional lipoma-** common, mature white fat
- **Hibernoma -** brown fat instead of the usual white fat
- **Fibrolipoma-** fat plus fibrous tissue
- **Angiolipoma -** fat plus a large amount of blood vessels
- **Myelolipoma-** fat plus tissue that makes blood cells
- **Spindle cell lipoma-** fat with cells that look like rods
- **Pleomorphic lipoma-** fat with cells of all different shapes and sizes
- **Atypical lipoma-** A deeper fat with a large number of cells

Treatment for Lipomas:

Observation

Since lipomas are benign tumors, there may not be a treatment option, depending on your symptoms. If you choose no treatment, it is very important that you see your doctor for regular visits to monitor any chances in the tumor.

Excision (Removal)

The only treatment that will completely remove a lipoma is a simple surgical procedure called excision.

- **Procedure-** In this procedure, a local anesthetic is typically injected around the tumor to numb the area. Large lipomas or those that are deep may require regional anesthesia or general anesthesia. Regional numbs a large area by injecting numbing medicine into specific nerves. General anesthesia puts you to sleep.

- **Recovery-** You should be able to go home soon after the procedure. You will have a few stitches, which your doctor will remove within a couple of weeks. How long it takes you to return to most daily activities will depend on the size and location of your lipoma. If you have any pain or discomfort, you may want to limit some activity. Your doctor will provide you with specific instructions to guide your recovery.

- **Recurrence-** Lipomas are almost always cured by simple excision. It is unusual for a lipoma to grow back, but if it does recur, excision is again the best treatment option.

Tests:

- X-ray
- Computed tomography
- Magnetic resonance imaging scans
- Biopsy
- Liposarcoma

Yes There Is Hope

Throw what you know, 'til you know what to throw. -Stephanie Wedgeworth

Never judge a book by its cover. -Nikki Hipple

My favorite quote is, 'When life throws you lemons make lemonade.' -Ana Diaz-Rincon

Singer Bob Marley said, 'You never know how strong you are until being strong is the only choice you can have.' -Marissa Jennifer Kulbacki

Randy Snow, a Paralympic tennis star said, 'I've never lost a single match; I've just run out of time fighting for a win.' -Tim Brumbalow

Singer Bob Marley said, 'Live the life you love and love the life you live.' -Brianna Cannon

Author Ralph Waldo Emerson said, 'I may not remember what you said to me, I may not remember what you did for me, but I will never forget how you made me feel." -T.Z.M

Faith is confidence in what we hope for and assurance about what we do not see. -Hallie Van Lare- Hurst

But the Lord said to Samuel, "Do not look at his appearance or at height of his stature, because I have rejected him; for God sees not as man sees, for man looks at the outward appearance, but the Lord looks at the heart." (1 Samuel 16:7) this verse has always been a favorite of mine, but ever since my boys were diagnosed with SB, it is especially close to my heart. We have had the opportunity to meet people with such diverse abilities ever since we had jack and Woody, and we can now look at people more like God sees them —as unique souls. -Mariann Noonan Wilson

I have always tried to remember with my daughter, to focus on what she can do instead of what she cannot do. -Jessica Padgett

CHAPTER 20

SKIN INTEGRITY BREAKDOWN

Skin care is very important because the skin is the largest organ of the human body. People with Spina Bifida can develop sores, calluses, blisters, and burns on their feet, ankles, and hips due to loss of sensation below the level of the spinal lesion. There may be partial or complete lost of normal skin sensitivity to pain, touch and temperature. Areas of affected skin also heal more slowly than areas with normal sensation. As a result individuals with Spina Bifida are at risk for injury to their skin from many sources including extremes of temperature and pressure.

Care must be taken to protect the skin from frostbite in the cold months and from burns from common sources such as hot bath water, radiators, and sunbaked blacktop. Redness and open areas, or pressures sores, can occur when the blood supply to the skin is cut off for more than ten minutes at a time. Pressure can be caused by not shifting weight frequently while sitting, using an improper wheelchair cushion, and wearing braces or shoes that don't fit well.

Abrasions may occur with crawling on the rug or floor. If damaged skin is not treated early, deeper layers of the skin can become involved and serious infection of the skin or underlying bones may develop. It is important that good skin care and careful inspection of the skin be learned in early childhood and become part of a lifelong self-care routine.

Protecting and caring for the skin:

Children:

- Checking the child skin regularly for redness, including under braces.
- Trying to avoid hot bath water, hot irons and hot unpadded seatbelts clasps that may cause burns.
- Making sure the child wears properly fitting shoes and socks at all times.
- Using sunscreen on the child and making sure the child doesn't stay out in the sun too long.
- Making sure the child does not sit or lie in one position for too long.
- Looking for red spots or areas of breakdown.
- Keeping hydrated can help skin remain healthy.
- Using a moisturizer daily.

- Changing wet or soiled pull-ups or clothing immediately.
- After soiling, wash skin with soap and water and apply a skin protecting cream.
- Move your body around every 15-30 minutes. Shake your arms above your head. Lift yourself up in your wheelchair using your arms to lift you and shift your weight.
- Follow a daily home exercise program to improve circulation.
- Keep body weight on the thinner side

Teens:

- Check skin every day for cuts, bruises, scratches, swelling, red marks
- Use large hand mirror to look at areas you can't see
- Always check water temperature before showering or bathing
- Avoid using creams and gels on irritated skin
- Be careful with any items that has been heated
- Apply sunscreen before spending time in the sun
- Wear socks and shoes when awake and up and about
- Don't smoke

- Eat healthy
- Drink plenty of water
- Avoid latex as preventive measures
- Perform wheelchair pushups and shift body weight

Adults:

- Check skin often
- Shift body in wheelchair to avoid pressure sores
- Wearing pressure stocking will help if feet become red or purple
- Look out for signs of insensate skin
  -Lack of feeling
  -Poor circulation
  -Inability to sweat
  -Bruising and slowness in healing

Marks you should look for:

- Pressure sores and scratches
- Rug burns and sunburns
- Red marks and rashes
- Bruises and calluses
- Abrasion and blisters
- Flea/bug bites
- Sunburns
- Rashes
- Pressure ulcers

Yes There Is Hope

My favorite bible verse is, 'I will praise you because I am fearfully and wonderfully made; your works are wonderful I know that full well.' (Psalm 139:14) -Kaylene Pilgram

My favorite bible verse is, 'By his stripes we are healed!' (Isaiah 53:5) -Vanessa Williams

My favorite bible verse is, 'When you go through the deep waters, I will be with you.' (Isaiah 43:2) -Tisha Pittman-Latson

My favorite bible verse is, 'And without faith it is impossible to please him, for whosoever would draw near God must believe that he exists and that he rewards those who seek him.' (Hebrews 11:6) -Dondre Wiggley

My favorite bible verse is, 'Jesus heals a man born blind.' (John 9:1-41) -Sly Bray

My name is Janice Knowles and I am the mother of a heroic son name Ron Eric Knowles. He is 31 years old now and because of him I found Jesus Christ. Since January 21, 1984, I have told everyone we meet, Ron was our one way ticket to heaven and with that I must say we are one of the fortunate parents to have had a child with Spina Bifida.

My favorite verse is, 'be still and know that I am God' (Psalms 46:10) -Mindy Rose

My favorite bible verse is, 'For I know the plans I have for you, "declares the Lord, "Plans to prosper you and not to harm you, plans to give you hope and a future.' (Jeremiah 29:11) -Joseph Gesse

My favorite bible verse is, 'I can do all things through Christ that strengthens me.' (Philippians 4:13) -Elizabeth Masoner Graham

Improvise. Adapt. Overcome. -Michael Turnbull

CHAPTER 21

PRECOCIOUS PUBERTY

Puberty is the time during which sexual and physical characteristics mature. Precocious puberty is when these body changes happen earlier than expected. Hormones control the timing and sequence of puberty. The age of onset of puberty varies from child to child but, in the United States, it usually begins in girls at 10 to 11 years of age and 11 to 12 years in boys.

Puberty often begins early in children with abnormalities of the central nervous system, family history of the disease, or rare genetic syndromes including those with Spina Bifida and hydrocephalus. This condition is known as Precocious Puberty. Tumors or growth of the ovaries may also be the cause of early puberty and sexual development in children. It may start before the age of 8 for girls and 9 for boys. About 1 in 5,000 children are affected. When puberty occurs, growth stops in the long bones of the arms and legs. Most children with this disorder grow fast at first, but also finish growing before reaching their full genetic height potential therefore, causing the individuals to be shorter than average.

Afro-Caribbean children tend to reach puberty earlier than Caucasian children. Diet and nutrition also affect the timing of puberty. Girls today reach puberty 2-3 years earlier than 100 years ago. This is thought to be largely due to better nutrition today. There are medications that can be used to delay the start of puberty to a more appropriate time. A full evaluation by a specialist (usually and endocrinologist-a doctor specializing in the diagnosis and treatment of disorder of glands) must be done to determine if this treatment is right for an individual child.

Sign of Precocious puberty:

Girls:

- Breast development
- Pubic or underarm hair
- Rapid height growth-a growth "spurt"
- Widening of the hips
- Onset of menstruation/ovulation
- Acne
- "Mature" body odor
- Increased aggression
- Typical moodiness associated with the hormonal changes

Boys:

- Enlargement of the testicles of penis
- Pubic, under arm, or facial hair
- Rapid height growth a-growth "spurt"
- Voice deepening
- Spontaneous erections
- Production of sperm
- Acne
- "Mature" Body odor
- Increased aggression
- Typical moodiness associated with the hormonal changes

Diagnosed for Precocious puberty:

- X-ray
- MRI
- Ultrasound
- Blood test
- A family history
- Physical exam

Treatment for early puberty:

- Nasal sprays
- Implants
- Injections
- Progestin
- Other treatment

Treatment considerations for Precocious puberty:

- Time since diagnosis
- Age
- Overall health
- Medical history
- Rate of development
- Current height
- Emotional maturity
- Child's tolerance for medications, procedures, or therapies
- Treating the underlying cause or disease, such as tumor
- Lowering the high levels of sex hormones with medication to stop sexual development from progressing

Yes There Is Hope

When I was born in Dec. 1965 doctors told my parents that I wouldn't see ten days or would be in a "Vegetative state". I am 49 years and by no means in a "vegetative state! -Peter Rutt

John Quincy Adams said, 'patience and perseverance have a magical effect before which difficulties disappear and obstacles vanish'. -A.T.

Normal is only a setting on the dryer. -Danielle Shearer

My favorite bible verse is, 'A time to love and a time to hate. A time for war and a time for peace'. (Ecclesiastes 3:8) -Joseph Brown

When one door closes unlock ten more windows of opportunity and possibilities will come flying through! -Nicole Springs

I live by the famous quote of William Shakespeare, "This above all; to thine own self be true."

My favorite bible verse is, 'Trust in the Lord with all your heart. Do not lean on your own understanding. In all your ways acknowledge him, and he will direct your paths'. (Proverbs 3:5-6) -David Brown

My favorite bible passage is, 'For I know the thoughts that I think towards you, saith the Lord, thoughts of peace, and not evil, to give you an expected end. Then shall ye call upon me, and ye shall go and pray unto me, and I will harken unto you. And ye shall seek me, and find me, when ye shall search for me all your heart. And I will be found of you, saith the Lord: and I will turn away your captivity, and I will gather you from the nations, and from all the places whither I have driven you, saith the Lord; and I will bring you again into the place whence I caused you to be carried away from captive.' (Jeremiah 29:11-14) -C.S.

Albus Dumbledore said, "It is not our abilities that show what we truly are, it is our choice." - Greg Chamberlain

If God brought you to it He will bring you through it. -Ryan Tometich

CHAPTER 2

SEXUAL FUNCTION

The nerves responsible for sexual sensation and function come from the lower portion of the spinal cord. As a result, most individuals with Spina Bifida will have some degree of sexual dysfunction. Females do not usually have sensation in the clitoris and, therefore, orgasms can also be affected with intercourse. However, they frequently have increased sensitivity in areas besides the genitalia and can have satisfying sexual lives. Fertility is normal and many women with Spina Bifida have families.

Those with high levels of paralysis may have severe curvature of the spine (scoliosis), small abdominal cavities, or other physical problems, may make it difficult to carry a child for a full nine months. In addition, vaginal births will be difficult for those women due to changes in the pelvic nerves and muscles. A gynecologist knowledgeable about Spina Bifida should be consulted when childbearing decisions are made. They will also be able to provide up-to-date information on the recommended dose of folic acid. Like their able-bodied peers, adult women with Spina Bifida require yearly gynecological examination and should be screened for breast and cervical cancer.

Some males with Spina Bifida can have erections, while others suffer from nerve damage or loss of sensation in the penis due to the level of paralysis. Ejaculation, or the discharge of sperm, does not always occur as it should and males may have issues fathering children. A sexual therapist or knowledgeable urologist can offer treatment to assist with both erection difficulties and infertility. As with all sexually active individuals, those with Spina Bifida are responsible for protecting themselves against unwanted pregnancy, AIDS and other sexually transmitted diseases. If you are using condoms, latex free are available from Durex. Latex Sheepskin condoms will not protect against AIDS.

New products which are both latex free and do protect against sexually transmitted disease are available. Consultation with a nurse or physician to determine the most appropriate form of birth control is recommended.

Major obstacles to a happy sex life are:

- Lack of confidence and self esteem
- Not meeting people
- No car
- Not seeing sex as being possible
- Incontinence
- Gaining independence from your parents

Why don't most men have sex as often as they could?:

- Urinary and bowel incontinence
- Difficulty with erections and/or positioning for sexual activity
- Delay in receiving sexual education
- Lack of social interaction/opportunity
- Low self esteem
- Lower overall neurologic function, which may be due to hydrocephalus
- Lack of independence from parents or caregivers

Treatment options for male erectile dysfunction:

- Medication
- Injections
- Pellets
- Pumps

- Implants
- Viagra pills

Treatment options for female:

Some women with Spina Bifida may have experience a loss of vaginal muscle control and is unable to produce natural vaginal lubrication.

- Water-based lubricates
- Devices such as (vibrators, clitoral vacuum)
- Estrogen therapy
- Androgen therapy

Contraception:

- Latex-free condoms
- Birth control
- Folic acid supplementation

Medical Screening:

- Breast cancer screening
- PAP smears
- Human Papilloma Virus (HPV) Vaccine

Yes There Is Hope

Live life, like there's no tomorrow and always follow your dreams. -S.W.

Never let anyone tell you a person with Spina Bifida can't do anything, I have Spina Bifida. - Mark Anderson

His disciples asked him, "Rabbi, who sinned, this man or his parents, that he was blind?" Neither this man nor his parents sinned," said Jesus, "but this happened so that the works of God might be displayed in him. (John 9:2-3)

A black belt is a white belt who never gave up. Criptaedo fans ROCK!!! -Paul Brailer founder of Criptaedo

Love is patient, love is kind. It does not envy, it does not boast, it is not proud. It does not dishonor others, it is not self-seeking, it is not easy angered, it keeps no record of wrongs. Love does not delight in evil but rejoices with truth. It always protects, always trusts, always hopes, always perseveres. Love never fails. But where there are prophecies, they will cease; where there are tongues, they will be still; where there is knowledge, it will pass away. (1 Corinthians 13:4-8) -Melissa Rider's favorite bible verse

For God so loved the world that he gave his one and only Son, that whosoever believes in him shall not perish but have eternal life. For God did not send his Son into the world to condemn the world, but to save the world through him. (John 3:16) -Rachael Barrett favorite bible verse

I can do all things through Christ which strengthen me (Philippians 4:13). When you get down because or your disability, look around you can find someone that is in worse shape than you are. -Christie Ferguson Banks

"I don't consider myself disabled I'm differently abled so don't dis my ability." -Karly Bertram

Many daughters have done well, but you excel them all. (Proverbs 31:29) -Brandy Marie Griswold's favorite bible verse

Never give up, don't let anyone boss you around. -C.M.

Spina Bifida can be a very challenging disability to deal with. Usually there are other neurological and physical conditions that go with it that involves multiple surgeries to correct or improve. But for me, keeping a positive attitude and surrounding myself with people who are loving and supportive is key to living a "normal" life. My life motto is: What doesn't kill you makes you stronger. -D.V.

CHAPTER 23

SCHOOLING FOR KIDS WITH SPINA BIFIDA

Many children with Spina Bifida do well in school. Yet some can experience difficulties at school. All children with Spina Bifida do not learn in the exact same way, especially children with shunts that are used to treat hydrocephalus (often called water on the brain). These children often have problems with learning due to short-term memory and poor organization skills. They may also have trouble making decisions. There are many activities that children can do both at home and at school to help solve these problems. Healthcare professionals can provide information about these activities.

Although some children with Spina Bifida will do well in regular classrooms without any special assistance, many will need support services in order to attend regular classes. Others will do best in a special educational setting. It is important that the abilities of each individual child be professionally assessed as early as possible, usually between the ages of two and five years. Psychological and neuropsychological strengths and weaknesses should be evaluated.

Federal and state laws including the Americans with Disabilities Act (ADA) and Public laws 94-142 and 99-457 require that individuals with disabilities be able to live, work and go to school in the least restrictive environment and receive those services necessary to help them benefit from their educational setting. It is important that parents be familiar with the various types of school programs available and, armed with the results of their child's psychological tests, advocate for appropriate placement. School entry can be made easier if parents meet with teachers and school personnel before classes begin.

Evaluation test:

- Intelligence testing is one of the primary tools for identifying children with mental retardation and learning disabilities.

- Academic testing provides a comprehensive approach to evaluate individuals who have specific learning disabilities or dyslexia or are gifted and talented. After the diagnostic evaluation, a prescriptive instructional plan is created and progress can be monitored.

- Visual motor testing assesses how a person can coordinate visually guided by fine-motor movements to be able to copy a design while it is in sight. Ages are from 0-3 years to 90+years.

Other test that may be given:

- Language ability appropriate social communication requires that children have adequate language to support their social interactions.
- Learning skills are often called the four C's: Critical thinking, creative thinking, communicating, and collaborating. These skills help students learn, so they are vital to success in school and beyond.
- Social/emotional functioning includes the child's experience, expression, and management of emotions and the ability to establish positive and rewarding relationships with others. It encompasses both intra- and interpersonal process.

What is an Individualized Education Program (IEP) or section 504 plan?:

Each public school child who receives special education and related services must have an Individualized Education Program (IEP). The IEP is a plan or program developed to ensure that a child who has a disability identified under the law and is attending an elementary or secondary educational institution receives specialized instruction and related services. The IEP creates an opportunity for teachers, parents, school administrators, related services personnel and students (when appropriate) to work together to improve educational results for children with disabilities. The IEP is the cornerstone of a quality education for each child with a disability.

The 504 plan is a plan developed to ensure that a child who has a disability identified under the law and is attending and elementary or secondary educational institution receives accommodations that will ensure their academic success and access to the learning environment.

Weaknesses and helping children with Spina Bifida:

- Handwriting- Children with Spina Bifida often have poor hand/eye coordination which makes handwriting a laborious task, physical and occupational therapy may be recommended to help develop these skills

- Mathematics- some children and adults with Spina Bifida meningomyelocele and hydrocephalus often have problems with any forms of math. While spelling and word recognition are sometimes well tasked math is the most academic challenge. Mathematics difficulties may be directly related to the thinning of the parietal lobes (regions implicated in mathematical functioning) and indirectly associated with deformities of the cerebellum ad midbrain that affects other functions involved in mathematical skills.

- Perceptual motor problem- Children with shunted hydrocephalus often have problems with eye-hand (visual-motor) activities. Visual perception problems mean the child may have problems "seeing "things in their head, finding their way around, and generally being less coordinated. Find-motor skills are often rather poor among Spina Bifida children. Together these weaknesses typically interfere with the ability to move around, use materials or tools and perform academics such as reading, arithmetic and writing.

- Language/Speech therapy- Intended to help children develop their speaking skills, as well as their abilities to understand and produce language. A speech language pathologist the therapist qualified to provide speech language therapy might work with a two year old who is not combining single words into short phrases. On some early intervention team the speech language pathologist may also help with feeding difficulties.

- Sequencing problems- Children and adolescents with Spina Bifida often have trouble keeping ideas or doing activities in their proper order. This problem may be related to not paying attention, not remembering or not being organized. The result is the same the child, parent and/or teacher begin to feel confused and frustrated because the steps are there just mixed up. It may also seem that the child or adolescent doesn't understand or comprehend the situation or question. These sequencing (ordering) problems can be seen in the school subjects of math and written language. It is also seen in not being able to tell time and count change. The young person can verbally tell a good story or report what they've seen in an orderly way until they have to write it down. They cannot organize (sequence) the idea in their head.

- Comprehension- children with Spina Bifida sometimes have a hard time understanding things even though they seem to understand. This is particularly true of some kids who speak well, but when they have to explain what they said, or respond to questions, they seem disorganized, and talk about irrelevant things. They may change the subject in the middle of what they are trying to say. This problem usually goes away by the time the child is about 10 years old but comprehension problems often go beyond this age. When it goes beyond this time, working to make it better is difficult. Several strategies can be used to help children who are having trouble understanding.

- Attention- it is quite common for children with Spina Bifida to have trouble paying attention to parents, teachers, friends, tasks, etc. This at times gets mixed up with a child being emotionally self-centered and not being attentive to other people's needs. Both may be true. Inattention, however, is particularly a problem in school. Children may miss assignments, miscopy assignments or work, generally be slow in completing work (beyond visual-motor speed problems), or miss social cues from others. Children with Spina Bifida generally are better able to pay attention when listening than when seeing.

- Memory- Children with Spina Bifida often have difficulty in remembering things they see or hear. Even if they understand it, they may not remember it later. So it's like they have to learn it over and over again. This can happen when people are telling them things to do or when they are copying assignments from the board. It seems hard to remember one thing, while they're trying to do another.

- Organization- Children with Spina Bifida may have trouble keeping things in organized. This is clearly seen when school materials, Paper, etc. need to be in order.

Things tend to get lost or misplaced, creating frustration, anxiety, and anger among parents, teachers, and even the child, at times.

• Understanding directions- Children with Spina Bifida sometimes have difficulties understanding directions. Some children benefit from seeing picture clues while others may need written notes, diagrams, and graphs to assist with understanding.

• Hyperactivity/Impulsivity- Children with Spina Bifida often exhibit restlessness and are fidgety, it is often surprising to teachers or even parents who think since orthopedic disability slows the child down, they can't be hyperactive. Yet this is not surprising when one is aware of visual-motor problems. While the physical impairment may mask the restlessness, it is often present. Also associated with inattention and hyperactivity is impulsivity. Children who are impulsive act before they think. This lack of stopping and thinking often gets them into trouble because they are doing things quickly and carelessly.

- Decision Making/Problem Solving- As you can image, if any person has trouble paying attention, remembering information, organizing things and keeping ideas in order, they will probably have difficulty making decisions and solving problems. Making a decision is a different process from solving a problem. One makes a decision when he/she has two or three choices and has to choose one of them, for example, what to eat or what to wear. Solving a problem usually means that you have a situation that requires you to use what you've learned in the past to solve a new problem now.

Yes There Is Hope

I always tell parents of kids with Spina Bifida to never underestimate the abilities of their child he/she can still accomplish anything. They can drive, go to college, have great meaningful relationships, have a great job and play sports if they put their mind to it. Anything is possible. -C.B.

I can do all things through Christ who give me strength. (Philippines 4:13) -Kristen Baker's favorite bible verse

Spina Bifida is not a disease it is a disability. -Jessa Hyde

I would say that, anything is possible. Obstacles and challenges in life make us stronger. Never give up, love who you are and go after your dreams with perseverance and an attitude of positivity! -Lila Hart

All creatures great and small God made them all. -Coleen Allen

My niece Hailee has Spina Bifida. She is an amazing child. She is loving and caring and has been through a lot and through it all she stays strong. -Connie Pescherine

Don't limit yourself. Many people limit themselves to what they think they can do. You can go as far as your mind lets you. What you believe, remember, you can achieve. -Alicia Fortner's favorite quote by Mary Kay Ash founder of Mary Kay Cosmetics Inc.

Trust in the Lord with all your heart and he shall direct your path. (Proverbs 3:5-6) -Sarah Merlau's favorite bible verse

I have Spina Bifida. I am 36 years old and I believe there is nothing I can't do. Positive attitude is everything. -AJR

I will tell you that you can do anything. Do not give up on your dreams. Keep your head up. -Virginia Vance

CHAPTER 24

SOCIAL SKILLS PROBLEM IN KIDS WITH SPINA BIFIDA

Young children with Spina Bifida are often able to cope relatively well with the condition. Problems tend to develop as a child gets older and they begin to mix with other children. During this period, children become more aware of how their condition makes them different from other children. It is normal for growing children to feel self-doubt or fear about how well they fit in with their peer group, and it is desirable that children with Spina Bifida not only socialize with children without disabilities, but they also have a chance to socialize and talk to other children with disabilities to share experiences.

Some children with Spina Bifida become reserved and withdrawn, while others begin to exhibit challenging behavior due to a sense of anger or frustration. Many children with hydrocephalus have problems with learning that makes it challenging to pick up verbal and non-verbal cues that is necessary for the acquisition of social skills. Children that have problems with non-verbal cues also have problems with perceiving intonation. Encouraging your child to participate in activities with other children can help boost their confidence and self-esteem.

Concerns parents of social need children have:

1. Talking over differences without getting angry
2. Persistence when facing frustration
3. Refusing request politely
4. Taking turns while talking
5. Understanding rules
6. Following directions
7. Waiting when necessary

Symptoms of non-verbal that involve social skills:

- Talk too much
- Shares information in inappropriate ways
- Relies on adults to get information
- Doesn't understand facial expressions
- Is overly literal and doesn't get riddles and sarcasm
- Withdraws from conversation with peers
- Prefers talking to adults rather than other kids

Getting help for non-verbal social skills:

- Talk to child teacher
- Look into educational evaluation
- Talk to your child doctor
- Talk to a specialist
- Talk to a learning specialist

Ways to improve social skills:

- Fight shyness
- Get involved in conversation
- Build self esteem
- Converse with people while carrying out daily activities
- Be relaxed and casual around people
- Gather the company of strong, well intentioned people who you or share your interests.
- Be kind to others
- Reference social skills books and guides
- Cultivate your sense of humor
- Choose specific goals and work towards them
- Select specific skills to improve
- Find people who share the same interests as you

Yes There Is Hope

Yea though I walk through I walk the valley of the shadows of death, I will fear no evil; for you are with me; your rod and your staff, they cover me. (Psalm 23:4) -Nick Hamburg's favorite bible verse

Love your children for who they are and teach them to be as independent as they can. -D.D.

When times get rough remember this one thing, there is no hill too steep for a climber. Literally when the curd hits the fan, just keep going. -N.L

Do not compare yourself to anyone. —Stari Schmidt favorite quote by Madra Jones

I can do all thing through Christ who gives me strengthens. (Philippians 4:13) -Kristina Hornback's favorite bible verse

The only thing that can stop you is your own mind. Go for yours. -Brandon C. Sims

Jesus wants me to cling to Him and rest until every care that I struggle with; I have placed in His hands. -Donna Powell

For thou hast possessed my reins: thou hast covered me in my mother's womb. I will praise thee; for I am fearfully and wonderfully made: marvellous are thy works; and that my soul knoweth right well. My substance was not hid from thee, when I was made in secret, and curiously wrought in the lowest parts of the earth. Thine eyes did see my substance, yet being unperfect; and in thy book all my members were written, which in continuance were fashioned, when as yet there was none of them. (Psalms 139:13-16) -Dani Herron's favorite bible verse

I have come that they may have life, and have it to the full. (John 10:10) -Gui's favorite bible verse

Do unto other what you would have them do unto you. (Luke 6:31) -Rose Gibson's favorite bible verse

CHAPTER 25

TRAVELING AND DISABILITIES

Preparing for your trip in advance will help to ensure that your travel is accessible, safe, and enjoyable. Each country has its own standards of accessibility for travelers with disabilities, and many countries do not require accommodations similar to what you might find in the United States.

Know before you go:

Preparation is critical. If you don't travel frequently, speak to someone with a similar disability who has traveled to your destination before. Consult your travel agent, hotel, airline, and others to understand the services available for the trip. Consider contacting disability organization overseas at www.miusa.org.

Fly Prepared:

The Transportation Security Administration (TSA) has a helpline number designed to assist travelers with disabilities and medical conditions. Travelers may call TSA Cares prior to traveling with questions about screening policies, procedures and what to expect at the security checkpoint. The Air Carrier Access Act and its amendments have result in the Department of Transportation (DOT) instituting regulations to ensure that persons with disabilities are treated without discrimination in ways consistent with the safe carriage of all passengers, domestically and internationally. Carriers are prohibited from imposing charges for providing required facilities, equipment, or services to an individual with a disability that is covered by DOT's Air Carrier Access regulations. Travelers with disabilities should review the department of Transportation pamphlet New Horizons for the Air Traveler with a Disability for more information about the Air Carrier Access Act.

Research Medical Care:

Consult with your physician prior to your travel overseas to identify your health are needs during your trip. Many countries have national health systems, but it is important to investigate availability and quality beforehand. Carry medical alert information and a letter from your health care provider describing your medical condition, medications, potential complications and other pertinent medical information.

Carry enough prescription medication to last your entire trip, including extra medicine in case you are delayed. Pack your medication in your carry-on bag, since checked baggage is occasionally lost. Always carry your prescription in their labeled containers, not in pill pack. Take a copy of your immunization records along in your hand-carry luggage.

Requirement for Service Dogs and Assistive Equipment:

Before you travel, contact the embassy or consulate of your destination country for information on possible restrictions for service dogs and assistive equipment. If service dogs are permitted, find out about requirements for quarantine, vaccination, and documentation. Talk with your vet about tips for traveling with a dog, and make sure your hotel will accommodate your service dog.

Find out if there are specific policies for devices such as wheelchairs, portable machines, batteries, respirators, and oxygen. You may want to research the availability of wheelchair and medical equipment providers in the areas you plan to visit.

Disabled travel tips:

- Call ahead
- Be specific and clear when describing a disability.
- Be specific and clear when describing the trip to your doctor.
- Take a doctor's note and phone number.
- Bring extra medication
- Avoid connecting flights
- Investigate physician availability where you are traveling.
- Know your right as a traveler with a disability.

Yes There Is Hope

My favorite Bible verse is Philippians 4:13, I can do all things through Christ who give me strength. -Mary Vannerson's favorite bible verse

Be completely humble and gentle, be patient, bearing with one another in love. (Ephesians 4:2) -Minnie Ford's favorite bible verse

Seek ye first the kingdom of God, and his righteousness; and all things shall be added unto you. (Matthew 6:33) -Stacey Able's favorite bible verse

For God so love the world that he gave his one and only Son, that whosoever believes in him shall not perish but have eternal life. (John 3:16) -Heaven Mccormick's favorite bible verse

He staggered not at the promise of God through unbelief; but was strong in faith, giving glory to God; and being fully persuaded that, what he had promised, he was able also to perform. And therefore it was imputed to him for righteousness. (Romans 4:20-22) -Brian Garcia's favorite bible verse

Isaiah 40:28 reads, 'Hast thou not known? Hast thou not heard, that the everlasting God, the Lord, the creator of the ends of the earth, fainteth not, neither is weary? There is no searching of his understanding.' -Valencia Brown

A time to be born and a time to die, a time to plant and a time to uproot, a time to kill and a time to heal, a time tear down and a time to build, a time to weep and a time to laugh, a time to mourn and a time to dance, a time to scatter stones and a time to gather them, a time to embrace and a time to refrain from embracing, a tie to search and a time to give up, a time to keep and a time to throw away, a time to tear and a time to mend, a time to be silent and a time to speak, a time to love and a time to hate, a time to war and a time for peace. (Ecclesiastes 3:2-8) - Pam Bechtel's favorite bible verse

He that dwelled in the secret place of the most high shall abide under the shadow of the Almighty. I will say of the Lord, He is my refuge and my fortress: my God in him will I trust. (Psalm 91:1-2) -Faith Reed's favorite bible verse

Weeping may endure for a night but joy cometh in the morning. (Psalms 30:50) -Donna Hamilton's favorite bible verse

CHAPTER 26

SAFETY

Safety is an important issue for children with Spina Bifida or any other disability. Children with disabilities sometimes have added challenges during an emergency situation compared to children without disabilities. They can be at a higher risk for injuries, bulling, abuse and assault. As these children become more independent, it is important for their parents and other family members to teach them how to stay safe and what to do if they feel threatened or have been hurt in any way. Keeping your family safe in an emergency situation starts in the home.

Some tips you can do are put a safety emergency kit together, sit down and make a family plan to do list in case of and emergency. Getting fire extinguishers and smoke detectors are a great thing to have in the home. Parents and caregivers can talk to their child's teachers, potential coaches or healthcare professionals about ways to keep him or her safe. You can also talk to your healthcare provider about the right equipment your child may need, as they get older.

Steps to keep children with disabilities safe:

- Learn about unique concerns and danger for the child
- Plan ways to protect child and share with others
- Remember that the child needs for protection will change over time

Basic items to put in safety emergency kit are:

- Flash Light
- Water one gallon per person, per day (3-day supply for evacuation, 2-week supply for home)
- First-aid kit
- Radio (hand cranked or battery powered)
- Extra batteries
- Food (non-perishable, easy to prepare items)
- Medications and medical items
- Multi- purpose items
- Baby supplies (bottle, diapers, formula, Baby food)
- Pet food and supplies
- Generator for home use
- Sanitation and personal hygiene items

- Copies of personal documents (Medication list and pertinent medical information, proof of address, deed/lease to home, passport, birth certificates, insurance policies)
- Cell phone with chargers
- Family and emergency contacts information
- Extra cash
- Emergency blankets
- Maps of the area

Making an emergency plan to do list:

- Teach child how to dial 911 in case of an emergency.
- Make diagram of home choose two place to meet:
  -Right outside your home in case of sudden emergency, such as a fire
  -Outside your neighborhood, in case you cannot return home or are asked to evacuate
- Decide where you would go and what route you would take to get there.
- Practice evacuating your home twice a year.
- Choose an out of area emergency contact person.
- Plan ahead for your pets.

- Teach a child to only go with someone who knows a secret "password" or "code word." This word can be anything, like a favorite color or food.

Yes There Is Hope

Be proud of who you are and what you have accomplished. Always try new things. Never say, "I can't" Unless you try to do it first. -Carl Malchoff

"Differently-abled is not the same as DIS-abled" -GaQuilla Hunter-Mathews

My Father said to me if there's ever a time to pray now is the time. I feel with lots of support and knowing people who have gone through finding out there baby have Spina Bifida we all will do our best to stay strong. Never be afraid to reach out for people who have dealt with it, when I finally did I felt a lot better. My biggest thing at this point with my unborn son is feeling those amazing kicks and how strong his heartbeat is. Children are amazing and will overcome anything they have the opportunity to. God gave me this child for a reason just like everyone else, be strong but also don't be afraid to brake as long as you get back up. You have to belong to find your inner fighter. -Katee Allen

"And we know that all things work together for good to them that love God, to them who are called according to his purpose." (Romans 8:28)

My 21 year old daughter and I both live by this verse first we thought Spina Bifida was a tragedy, but so much good has come out of it; patience, love and hard work to name a few. - Stephanie Massey's favorite bible verse

The Lord is my shepherd; I shall not want. He makes me to lie down in green pastures; He leads me beside the still waters. He restores my soul; He leads me in the paths of righteousness For His name's sake. Yea though I walk through the valley of the shadow of death, I will fear no evil; For You are with me; Your rod and Your staff, they comfort me. You prepare a table before me in the presence of my enemies; You anoint my head with oil; My cup runs over. Surely goodness and mercy shall follow me all the days of my life; and I will dwell in the house of the Lord forever. (Psalm 23:1-6) -Kee Kee Cole's favorite bible verse

I can do all things through him who gives me strength. (Philippians 4:13) -Dan Mccoy's favorite bible verse

For God so love the world that he gave His only begotten Son, that whosoever believes in Him should not perish but have everlasting life. (John 3:16) -Brea Morrison's favorite bible verse

If anyone has material possessions and sees a brother or sister in need but has no pity on them, how can the love of God be in that person? Dear children, let us not love with words or speech but with actions and in truth. (1John 3:17-18) - Samantha Hives favorite bible verse

Do not be anxious about anything, but in every situation, by prayer and petition, with thanksgiving present your request to God. And the peace of God, which transcends all understanding, will guard your hearts and your minds in Christ Jesus. (Philippians 4:6-7) - Rachelle McCormick Flowers favorite bible verse

As a mom of a 15-month-old baby, I am still very new at things. Spina Bifida is a spectrum! Such as fun and frustrating, terrifying word spectrum! I am a "hope for the best, but plan for the worse" type of person. So we plan on helping my daughter accomplish anything she wants as she grows! The most rewarding thing in life requires some of the most work! -Lennel Krieck

For God so loved the world that he gave his one and only Son, that whoever believes in him shall not perish but have eternal life. - Shawntavia Burr

I can do all things through Christ that

strengthen me. -Antonio Orlina

I love having Deangelo as my brother. He is the strongest person I know. -Devonte McCormick

I'm thankful for having Deangelo in my life, because he's is the best brother ever. -Destiny McCormick

I love my brother Deangelo -Desiray McCormick

Deangelo is one of the most nonchalant, inspirational, funniest human beings I've ever known. Through his ups and downs you will never know how he is truly feeling because of his character. I'm honored that God has given me the opportunity to care for this bright young man that I call my son. –Dad

Kenida's top 20 Tips for parents with special needs children

1) Educate yourself about your child's special needs

2) Try to meet their every need.

3) Pay attention and listen to what your child is trying to tell you.

4) Allow them to be as independence as possible.

5) Being flexible is necessary with special needs children.

6) Take care of their feelings make them feel safe and secure.

7) Set goals for your child.

8) Be positive and consistent.

9) Always have a plan and a backup plan.

10) Don't minimize the need for some alone time for yourself.

11) Always make your child feel a part of different activities.

12) Treat your special needs child as much like their other siblings as possible.

13) Don't be afraid to ask for help when needed.

14) Make sure to have date nights or date mornings with significant other when needed.

15) Join parent support groups with families who are experiencing the same thing.

16) Remove all distractions.

17) Keep your sense of humor.

18) Give your child lots of love.

19) Celebrate the little things your special needs child accomplishes.

20) Enjoy life to the fullest

GLOSSARY

Adolescent- Growing to manhood or womanhood; youthful.

Ambulatory- Of relating to, or capable of walking.

Anaphylactic- Exaggerated allergic reaction to a foreign protein resulting from previous exposure to it.

Anesthesia- Insensitivity to pain, especially as artificially induced by the administration of gases or the injection of drugs before surgical operations

Anxiety- Distress or uneasiness of mind caused by fear of danger or misfortune.

Appendicectomy- Surgical removal of any appendage esp. the vermiform appendix

Anal Electromyography- Is an electrical recording of muscle activity that aids in the diagnosis of neuromuscular disease.

Anorectal Manometry- Measures the tone in the anal sphincter and rectal muscles.

Anorectal Ultrasound- An accepted modality for the evaluation of several conditions, including fecal incontinence, anal sepsis, and anal cancer.

Biopsy- The removal for diagnostic study of a piece of tissue from a living body

Caesarean section or (C-section)- A surgical procedure in which one or more incisions are made through a mother's abdomen and uterus to deliver one or more babies.

Calvarium- The dome of the skull.

Colonoscopy- An exam used to detect changes or abnormalities in the large intestine (colon) and rectum.

Colostomy- A surgical procedure in which an opening (stoma) is formed by drawing the healthy end of the large intestine or colon through an incision in the anterior abdominal wall and suturing it into place.

Computed tomography- Is an imaging procedure that uses special x-ray equipment to create a series of detailed pictures, or scans, of areas inside the body. It is also called computerized tomography and computerized axial tomography (CAT) scanning.

Conception- The process of becoming pregnant involving fertilization or implantation or both.

Constipation- Also known as costiveness or

dyschezia refers to bowel movements that are infrequent or hard to pass.

Conus Medullaris- The tapered, lower end of the spinal cord. It occurs near lumbar vertebral levels 1 (L1) and 2 (L2).

Cystomestrogram- Allows us to assess how your bladder and sphincter behave while you store urine and when you pass urine.

Cyst- A closed, bladder-like sac formed in animal tissues, containing fluid or semi fluid matter.

Defecography- Uses an X-ray to look at the shape and position of the rectum as it empties.

Depression- A condition of general emotional dejection and withdrawal; sadness greater and more prolonged than that warranted by any objective reason.

Diastematomyelia- A congenital disorder in which a part of the spinal cord is split, usually at the level of the upper lumbar vertebra.

Duramater- One of the membranes that sheathes the spinal cord and brain; the dura mater is the outermost layer.

Echogenic intracardiac focus (EIF)- A small bright spot seen in the baby's heart on an ultrasound exam.

Electromyogram (EMG)- Measures the electrical activity of muscles at rest and during contraction.

Embryo- An unborn or unhatched offspring in the process of development.

Endoscopy- Is a nonsurgical procedure used to examine a person's digestive tract.

Endosonogaphy- A device that generates sound waves is placed on the skin after a gel is applied to conduct the sound waves and allow examination of many organs of the body, including liver, kidneys, gallbladder, and ovaries.

Epilepsya- Disorder of the nervous system, characterized either by mild, episodic loss of attention or sleepiness (petit mal) or by severe convulsions with loss of consciousness (grand mal).

Fetus- An unborn offspring of a mammal, in particular an unborn human baby more than eight weeks after conception.

Folic Acid- Is a B vitamin. It helps the body make healthy new cells.

Gynecologist- Is the medical practice dealing with the health of the female reproductive systems (vagina, uterus and ovaries) and the breasts.

Hodgkins lymphoma- Cancer of the part of the immune system called the lymphatic system.

Intensive Care Unit (ICU)- Is a special department of a hospital or health care facility that provides intensive care medicine.

Incontinence- Is a lack of control.

Kidneys- Are bean-shaped organs that serve several essential regulatory roles in vertebrates.

Laminectomy- Is surgery that creates space by removing the lamina (the back part of the vertebra) that covers your spinal canal.

Laryngoscopy- Is an exam of the back of your throat, including your voice box (larynx). Your voice box contains your vocal cords and allows you to speak.

Liposarcomas- Are malignant tumours of fatty tissue and are the malignant counterpart to a benign lipoma.

Magnetic resonance imaging (MRI)- Is a noninvasive medical test that helps physicians diagnose and treat medical conditions. MRI uses a powerful magnetic field, radio frequency pulses and a computer to produce detailed pictures of organs, soft tissues, bone and virtually all other internal body structures.

Manual muscle testing- A procedure for the evaluation of the function and strength of individual muscles and muscle groups based on the effective performance of a movement in relation to the forces of gravity and manual resistance.

Muscle paralysis- loss of muscle function for one or more muscles. Paralysis can be accompanied by a loss of feeling (sensory loss) in the affected area if there is sensory damage as well as motor.

Myelogram- A diagnostic imaging procedure done by a radiologist. It uses a contrast dye and X-rays or computed tomography (CT) to look for problems in the spinal canal, including the spinal cord, nerve roots, and other tissues.

Myeloma- A cancer of plasma cells

Neural tube defect- A opening in the spinal cord or brain that occurs very early in human development.

Neuropsychological evaluation- An assessment of how one's brain functions, which indirectly yields information about the structural and functional integrity of your brain.

Neurosurgeon- Is a physician who specializes in the diagnosis and surgical treatment of disorders of the central and peripheral nervous system including congenital anomalies, trauma, tumors, vascular disorders, infections of the brain or spine, stroke, or degenerative diseases of the spine.

Neurological disorders- A disease of the brain, spine and the nerves that connect them.

Neurologist- The neurologist treats disorders that affect the brain, spinal cord, and nerves.

Nystagmus- A condition of involuntary eye movement, acquired in infancy or later in life, that may result in reduced or limited vision.

Occupational therapy (OT)- The use of assessment and treatment to develop, recover, or maintain the daily living and work skills of people with a physical, mental, or cognitive disorder.

Orthopaedic surgery- The branch of surgery concerned with conditions involving the musculoskeletal system.

Orthotist- The primary medical clinician responsible for the prescription, manufacture and management of orthoses.

Optic atrophy- A condition that affects the optic

nerve, which carries impulses from the eye to the brain.

Ophthalmologist- A specialist in medical and surgical eye problems.

Physical therapists- Help injured or ill people improve their movement and manage their pain.

Physicians- Diagnose, examine patients; take medical histories; prescribe medications; and order, perform, treat injuries or illnesses, and interpret diagnostic tests.

Physiotherapists- Experts in movement and function who work in partnership with their patients, assisting them to overcome movement disorders, which may have been present from birth, acquired through accident or injury, or are the result of ageing or life-changing events.

Pressure sore- Any redness or break in the skin caused by too much pressure on your skin for too long a period of time.

Pressure ulcers- Are localized injuries to the skin and/or underlying tissue that usually occur over a bony prominence as a result of pressure, or pressure in combination with shear and/or friction.

Psychological- Pertaining to the mind or to

mental phenomena as the subject matter of psychology.

Psychologist- Evaluates diagnoses, treats, and studies behavior and mental processes.

Seizures- The action of capturing someone or something using force.

Scoliosis- Abnormal lateral curvature of the spine.

Sigmoidoscopy- Examination of the sigmoid colon by means of a flexible tube inserted through the anus.

Sonographer- A highly skilled medical imaging professional within the allied health sector that operates an ultrasound machine to perform diagnostic medical Sonographic- examinations.

Specialist- A person who devotes himself or herself to one subject or to one particular branch of a subject or pursuit.

Speech pathologist- The study and treatment of human communication and its disorders.

Spinal canal- The space in vertebrae through which the spinal cord passes. It is a process of the dorsal body cavity.

Strabismus- Abnormal alignment of the eyes;

the condition of having a squint.

Syingomyelia- A chronic progressive disease in which longitudinal cavities form in the cervical region of the spinal cord. This characteristically results in wasting of the muscles in the hands and a loss of sensation.

Tethered spine- Refers to a group of neurological disorders that relate to malformations of the spinal cord.

Ultrasound/Ultrasonography- A test in which high-frequency sound waves (ultrasound) are bounced off tissues and the echoes are converted into a picture (sonogram).

Urostomy- Surgical construction of an artificial excretory opening from the urinary tract.

Ventriculomegaly- A brain condition that occurs when the lateral ventricles become dilated.

Vertebrae- Any of the bones or segments composing the spinal column, consisting typically of a cylindrical body and an arch with various processes, and forming a foramen, or opening, through which the spinal cord passes.

Voiding cystrourethogram- A technique for visualizing a person's urethra and urinary bladder while the person urinates (voids).

Xray- A form of electromagnetic radiation, similar to light but of shorter wave length and capable of penetrating solids and of ionizing gases.

National Family Resources

<u>ALABAMA</u>

Children's Hospital
Spina Bifida Clinic (pediatric-will refer adults with MMC)
1600 7th Avenue S.
Birmingham, AL 35233
Phone: 1-205-939-5281
Web: www.chsys.org

UAB Spain Rehab Adult Transition Clinic (for adults)
1717 Sixth Ave S
Birmingham, Alabama 35233
Phone: 1-205-934-4179
Web: www.uabmedicine.org

Children's Rehabilitation Services Spina Bifida Clinic (pediatric-will refer adults)
1610 Center Street, Suite A
Mobile, AL 36604
Phone: 1-251-432-4560
Web: http://www.rehab.state.al.us

ALASKA

The Children's Hospital at Providence (pediatric and adult)
3340 Providence Dr, Ste. A351
Anchorage, AK 99508
Phone: 1-907-212-4824
Web: www.providence.org/alaska/services

ARIZONA

Children's Clinic Rehabilitation Services (CCRS) (pediatric only)
2600 N Wyatt Drive
Tucson, AZ 85712
Phone: 1-520-324-3244
Web: www.childrensclinics.org/

DMG Children's Rehabilitative Services
3141 N. 3rd Avenue
Phoenix AZ, 85013
Phone: 1-602-914-1520
Web: www.dmgcrs.org

ARKANSAS

Arkansas Children's Hospital Spina Bifida Clinic/Program (pediatric only)
1 Children's Way, Mail Slot 650
Phone: 1-501-364-1806
Web: www.archildrens.org

CALIFORNIA

Children's Hospital of Los Angeles Spina Bifida Center (pediatric only-to age 21)
4560 Sunset Blvd.
Los Angeles, CA 90027
Phone: 1-323-361-2384
Web: www.childrenshospitalla.org

LAC + USC Medial Center Spina Bifida Clinic (pediatric-will refer adults)
1200 N. State St IRD rm 123
Los Angeles, CA 90033
Phone: 1-323-226-3691
Web: www.uscpediatrics.com

National Rehabilitation Center (pediatric and adult)
7601 Imperial Hwy., JPI 3145
Downey, CA 90242
Phone: 1-562-401-7111
Web: www.rancho.org

Children's Hospital and Research Center Oakland Spina Bifida Clinic (pediatric only)
747 52nd Street
Oakland, CA 94609
Phone: 1-510-428-3655
Web: www.childrenshospitaloakland.org

Miller Children's Hospital Myelomeningocele Center/Spina Bifida Center (pediatric only)
2801 Atlantic Avenue
Long Beach, CA 90806
Phone: 1-562-933-8832
Fax: 1-562-933-8844
Web: www.millerchildrenshospitallb.org/

Los Angeles Orthopaedic Medical Center Spina Bifida Department (pediatric only)
2400 S. Flower Street, 2nd Floor
Los Angeles, CA 90007
Phone: 1-213-741-8365
Web: www.orthohospital.org

Children's Hospital Central California Spina Bifida Clinic (pediatric and adult)
9300 Valley Children's Place,
Madera, CA 93636
Phone: 1-559-353-6786
Web: www.childrenscentralcal.org

Kaiser Permanente Spina Bifida Program (pediatric to age 23)
280 W. MacArthur Blvd.
Oakland, CA 94611
Phone: 1-510-752-6919
Web: www.genetics.kaiser.org

Children's Hospital Orange County (CHOC) Children's Hospital Spina Bifida Clinic (pediatric to age 21)
455 S. Main St.
Orange, CA 92868
Phone: 1-714-532-8497
Email: eab0@choc.org
Web: www.choc.org

Shriners Hospital for Children - Los Angeles Myelodysplasja Clinic (pediatric only)
3160 Geneva Street
Los Angeles, CA 90020
Phone: 1-213-368-3151
Web: www.shrinershospitalsforchildren.org

Shriners Hospital for Children – Northern California Spina Bifida Clinic (pediatric only)
2425 Stockton Blvd.
Sacramento, CA 95817
Phone: 1-916-453-2059
Web: www.shrinershq.org/Hospitals/Main/

Loma Linda University Children's Hospital Spina Bifida Team Center (pediatric to age 21)
2195 Club Center Dr., Ste G
San Bernardio, CA 92408
Phone: 1-909-835-1816
Email: vvasquez@llu.edu
Web: www.llu.edu/lluch/

Rady Children's Hospital Spinal Defects Clinic (pediatric only-will refer adults)
3020 Children's Way
San Diego, CA 92123
Phone: 1-858-966-8896
Web: www.rchsd.org

University of California San Francisco Benioff Children's Hospital Spina Bifida Clinic (pediatric only)
4000 Parnassus Ave.
505 Parnassus Avenue, BOX 0110
San Francisco, CA 94143
Phone: 1-415-476-3899
Web: www.ucsfhealth.org/childrens/

Santa Clara Valley Medical Center Pediatric Specialties Spina Bifida Clinic
750 S. Bascom Avenue
San Jose, CA 95128
Phone: 1-408-885-4780
Web: www.sccgov.org

COLORADO

The Children's Hospital Colorado Spinal Defects Clinic (pediatric to age 21)
13123 East 16th Ave.
Aurora, CO 80045
Phone: 1-720-777-3928
Web: www.thechildrenshospital.org

CONNECTICUT

Connecticut Children's Medical Center Spina Bifida Clinic (pediatric only)
282 Washington Street
Hartfort, CT 06106
Phone: 1-860-545-9100
Web: www.connecticutchildrens.org/

DELAWARE

AI Dupont Hospital for Children Nemours Children's Clinic Spina Dysfunction Program (pediatric only)
1600 Rockland Rd. P.O. Box 269
Wilmington, DE 19803
Phone: 1-302-651-5993
Web: www.nemours.org/clinic/de/wil.html

DISTRICT OF COLUMBIA

Children's National Medical Center Myelomeningocele and Other Spinal Cord Injuries Clinic (pediatric and adult)
111 Michigan Ave, NW
Washington, D.C. 20010
Phone: 1-202-476-3094
Web: www.dcchildrens.com

FLORIDA

Nemours Children's Clinic Spina Bifida Program (pediatric and adult)
807 Children's Way
Jacksonville, FL 32207
Phone: 1-904-390-3562
Web: www.nemours.org

Arnold Palmer Hospital /Spina Bifida Program (pediatric to age 21) Orlando Health MP358
83 W. Columbia St.
Orlando, FL 32806
Phone: 1-321-841-5683
Email: kayleen.ala@orlandohealth.com
Web: www.orlandohealth.com/

Shriner's Hospital for Children - Tampa Spina Bifida Clinic (pediatric only)
12502 N. Pine Drive
Tampa, FL 33612
Phone: 1-813-975-7137
Web: www.shrinershospitalsforchildren.org

GEORGIA

Children's Healthcare of Atlanta at Scottish Rite Judson Hawk Multi-Specialty clinic (pediatric-will refer adults)
5455 Meridian Mark Rd., Ste. 200
Atlanta, GA 30342
Phone: 1-404-785-4593
Web: www.choa.org

Shepherd Center Outpatient Clinic (adult and pediatric 13 years old and older)
2020 Peachtree Rd. NW
Atlanta, GA 30309
Phone: 1-404-352-2020
Web: www.shepherd.org

HAWAII

Shriners Hospital
Myelo Clinic (pediatric only)
1310 Punahou Street
Honolulu, HI 96826
Phone: 1-808-951-3704
Web: www.shrinershq.org/hospitals/honolulu/

IDAHO

St. Luke's Children's Specialty Center
Myelo Clinic (pediatric and adult)
100 E. Idaho Ste. 200
Boise, ID 83712
Phone: 1-208-381-7122

ILLINOIS

Ann & Robert H. Lurie Children's Hospital of Chicago Spina Bifida Center (pediatric to age 25)
2515 N. Clark
Chicago, IL 60614
Phone: 1-312-227-5340
Web: www.luriechildrens.org

Rehabilitation Institute of Chicago (adults only)
345 Superior Street
Chicago, IL 60611
Phone: 1-312-238-1000
Web: www.ric.org

Shriners Hospital for Children Myelomeningocele Clinic (pediatric-will refer adults)
2211 N. Oak Park Avenue
Chicago, IL 60707
Phone: 1-773- 622-5400
Web: www.shrinershospitalsforchildren.org/

Lutheran General Children's Hospital Spina Bifida Clinic, 3rd floor, Yackman Pavillion
1675 Dempster Street
Park Ridge, IL 60068
Phone: 1-847-723-5065
Web: www.advocatehealth.com

St Francis Hospital INI
Spina Bifida Clinic (pediatric and adult)
420 N.E. Glen Oak, Suite 201
Peoria, IL 61603
Phone: 1-309-655-3800
Web: www.osfsaintfrancis.org

INDIANA

Riley Hospital for Children at Indiana
University Health Myelomeningocele
Program (pediatric-will refer adults)
705 Riley Hospital Drive, RI 1610
Indianapolis, IN 46202
Phone: 1-317-944-4846
Email: LLowe@iupui.edu
Web: www.iuhealth.org/riley/

St. Joseph's Regional Medical Center
Pediatric Specialty Clinics (pediatric-will
refer adults)
611 E Douglas Ste. 405
Mishawaka, IN 46545
Phone: 1-574- 335-6240
Web: www.sjmed.com

IOWA

Alfred Healy Clinic
Center for Disabilities and Development
(pediatric and adult)
100 Hawkins Drive
Iowa City, IA 52242-1011
Phone: 1-877-686-0031
Phone: 1-319-353-6900
Web: www.healthcare.uiowa.edu/

KANSAS

University of Kansas Hospital
Spina Bifida Clinic (pediatric and adult)
3901 Rainbow Blvd.,
Kansas City, KS 66160
Phone: 1-913- 588-5939
Email: astanton@kumc.edu
Web: www.kumc.edu

Special Health Care Services Spinal Cord
Clinic Wesley Medical Arts Tower Building
(pediatric-will refer adults)
3243 Murdock, Level G
Wichita, KS 67214
Phone: 1-316-962-2021

KENTUCKY

**Shriner's Hospital for Children
Spina Bifida Program (ortho clinic only-
will refer for pediatric and adult care)**
1900 Richmond Road
Lexington, KY 40502
Phone: 1-859- 268-5742
Web: www.shriners.net

**KY Commission for Children with Special
Health Care Needs (pediatric-will refer
adults)**
310 Whittington Parkway, Suite 200
Louisville KY 40222
Phone: 1-502- 429-4489
Phone: 1-800- 232-1160
Web: http://chfs.ky.gov/ccshcn/

**Frazier Rehab Institute Adult Spina Bifida
Clinic (Adults Only)**
220 Abraham Flexner Way
Louisville, KY 40202
Phone: 1-502-582-7495

LOUISIANA

**Shriners Hospital for Children (pediatric
only)
Spina Bifida Program**
3100 Samford Avenue
Shreveport, LA 71103
Phone: 1-318-222-5704
Web: www.shriners.net

MAINE

Maine Medical Partners Pediatric Specialty Care Spina Bifida Program (pediatric and adult)
1577 Congress St., 2nd Floor
Portland, ME 04102
Phone: 1-207-662-5522, Option 8, Option 7
Email: mcevoa@mmc.org
Web: http://www.mmc.org/

MARYLAND

**Kennedy Krieger Institute
The Keelty Center for Spina Bifida and Related Disorders (pediatric and adult)**
707 N. Broadway,
Baltimore, MD 21205
Phone: 1-443-923-9130
Email: SpinaBifidaCenter@KennedyKrieger.org
Web: http://www.kennedykrieger.org

MASSACHUSETTS

**Children's Hospital
Myelodysplasia Clinic (pediatric and adult)**
300 Longwood Ave., Fegan 3
Boston, MA 02115
Phone: 1-617-355-7704
Web: www.childrenshospital.org/

Massachusetts Hospital School (DPH) (pediatric only, ages 7 to 22)
3 Randolph Street
Canton, MA 02021
Phone: 1-781-828-2440
Web: www.MHSF.us

Shriner's Hospital for Children Myelodysplasia Clinic (pediatric only)
516 Carew Street
Springfield, MA 01104
Phone: 1-413-787-2088
Web: www.shrinershospitalsforchildren.org/

MICHIGAN

Children's Hospital of Michigan Myelomeningocele Care Center (pediatric to age 21)
3901 Beaubien
Detroit, MI 48201
Phone: 1-313-745-5226
Email: pbeierwa@dmc.org
Web: www.childrensdmc.org/pediatric-myelomeningocele-care

Mary Free Bed Rehabilitation Center
235 Wealthy SE
Grand Rapids, MI 49506
Phone: 1-616-242-0395
Phone: 1-800-668 6001
Web: www.maryfreebed.com

Sparrow Hospital
Sparrow Hospital Myelodysplasia Clinic
(pediatric and adult)
1200 E. Michigan Avenue, SPB Suite 460
Lansing, MI 48909
Phone: 1-517-364-5415
Web: www.sparrow.org

University of Michigan
Myelodysplasia Clinic (pediatric and adult
up to age 25)
1500 E. Medical Center Drive
Taubman 3552
Ann Arbor, MI 48109-5338
Web: www.med.umich.edu/healthcenters/clinics

UMHS Physical Medicine & Rehabilitation
325 E. Eisenhower, Box 0744 (pediatric only)
Ann Arbor, MI 48073
Phone: 1-734-936-7200
Web: www.med.umich.edu/rehabeng/index.htm

MINNESOTA

Park Nicollett Methodist Hospital
Minneapolis Spina Bifida Clinic
2001 Blaisdell Ave.
Minneapolis, MN 55404
Phone: 1-952-993-9100
Web: www.parknicollett.com

Shriners Hospital - Twin Cities
Spina Bifida Clinic (pediatric only)
2025 E. River Parkway
Minneapolis, MN 55414
Phone: 1-612-596-6128
Web: www.shrinershospitals.org

Mayo Clinic Spina Bifida Clinic (pediatric-will refer adults)
200 First St. SW
Rochester, MN 55905
Phone: 1-507-266-8404
Web: www.mayoclinic.org

Gillette Children's Specialty Healthcare
Gillette Lifetime Specialty Care Clinic
(adults only-age 16 and over)
435 Phalen Blvd.
St. Paul, MN 55130
Phone: 1-651-229-3878
Email: jwilhelmy@gillettechildrens.com
Web: www.gillettechildrens.org

Gillette Children's Specialty Healthcare
Center for Spina Bifida (pediatric only)
200 E University Avenue
St. Paul, MN 55101
Phone: 1-651-290-8712
Web: www.gillettechildrens.org

MISSISSIPPI

Mississippi State Department of Health
Blake Clinic for Children (pediatric only)
Jackson Medical Mall, Suite 454
350 Woodrow Wilson Drive
Jackson, MS 39213
1-601-987-3965
Web: www.msdh.state.ms.us/msdhsite

MISSOURI

Children's Mercy Hospital & Clinics
Spinal Defects Clinic (pediatric only-will
refer adults)
2401 Gillham Road
Kansas City, MO 64024
Phone: 1-816-234-3790
Phone: 1-816-234 3005
Web: www.childrens-mercy.org/

Cardinal Glennon Children's Medical
Center
Myelomeningocele Clinic (pediatric 0-30,
will refer older adults)
1465 South Grand Blvd.
St. Louis, MO 63104-1095
Phone: 1-314-268-2700 ext. 4178
Web: www.cardinalglennon.com

St. Louis Children's Hospital SB clinic (pediatric 0-25, will refer older adults)
One Children's Place
St. Louis, MO 63110
Phone: 1-314-454-5333
Web: www.StLouisChildrens.org

Shriner's Hospital for Children(pediatric only)
2001 S. Linberg Blvd.
St. Louis, MO 63131
Phone: 1-314-432-3600

MONTANA

Please check neighboring states.

NEBRASKA

State of Nebraska
MHCP Mid-Line Clinic (pediatric and adult)
412 S. Saddlecreek Rd.
Omaha, NE 68509
Phone: 1-402-471-9292
Web: www.dhhs.ne.gov/dip/dipindex.htm

Children's Hospital and Medical Center Children's Developmental Clinic (pediatric only)
8200 Dodge Street
Omaha, NE 68114-4114
Phone: 1-402-955-4160
Web: www.chsomaha.org

NEVADA

Please check neighboring states.

NEW HAMPSHIRE

**Dartmouth Hitchcock Medical Center
Spinal Dysraphism Program (pediatric and
adult up to age 25)**
Clinic 6L, One Medical Center Dr.
Lebanon, NH 03756
Phone: 1-603-653-9623
Web: http://chad.dartmouth- hitchcock.org/

NEW JERSEY

**Children's Specialized Hospital
Spinal Cord Dysfunction Clinic (pediatric-
will refer adults)**
150 New Providence Road
Mountianside, NJ 07092-2590
Phone: 1-908-233-3720

**Kessler Institute for Rehabilitation
1199 Pleasant Valley Way (adults only)**
West Orange, NJ 07052
Phone: 1-973-243-6999

NEW MEXICO

Carrie Tingley Hospital
SB/Myleo Clinic (pediatric - will refer adults)
1127 University Blvd., NE
MSC 074090
Albuquerque, NM 87102-1715
Phone: 1-505-272-5287
Web: http://hospitals.unm.edu/

NEW YORK

Hospital for Joint Diseases
Neuromuscular Clinic/Multi-Disciplinary Spina Bifida Clinic
301 E. 17th Street
New York, NY 14222
Phone: 1-716-888-1345
Web: www.wchob.org

Columbia University Medical Center
New York Presbyterian Medical Center
Neurologic Institute (No SB clinic-pediatric only)
710 W 168th
New York, NY 10032
Phone: 1-212-342-6867
Web: www.nyp.org

Strong Memorial Hospital
Andrew J. Kirch Developmental Services
Center (pediatric only)
601 Elmwood Avenue, Box 671
Rochester, NY 14642
Phone: 1-585-275-2986
Web: www.stronghealth.com

SUNY Upstate Medical University Hospital
Spina Bifida
Program/Neurodevelopmental Pediatrics
(pediatric only)
725 Irving Ave., Ste. 112
Physician's Office Building
Syracuse, NY 13210
Phone: 1-315- 464-5259
Web: www.upstate.edu/

Helen Hayes Hospital
Spinal Cord Clinic (adults only)
RT 9 W
West Haverstraw, NY 10993
Phone: 1-845-786-4297
Web: www.helenhayeshospital.org

NORTH CAROLINA

Olson Huff Center
11 Vanderbilt Park Drive (pediatric and adult-
referral required)
Asheville, NC 28803
Phone: 1-828-213-1780

Spina Bifida Clinic at UNC
Campus Box #7200 (pediatric and adult)
UNC School of Medicine
Chapel Hill, NC 27599
Phone: 1-919-966-8813

Terry Des Ravines
Levine Children's Specialty Center
Medical Center Plaza (pediatric only)
1001 Blythe Boulevard
Charlotte, NC 28203
Phone: 1-704-381-8855

Duke University Medical Center
Myelodysplasia Clinic (pediatric and adult)
3000 Erwin Road
Durham, NC 27710
Phone: 1-919-681-5456
Web: www.dukechildrens.org

Pitt Memorial Rehab Clinic
ECU-SOM, Department of Physical
Medicine and Rehab (pediatric and adult)
600 Moye Blvd.
Greenville, NC 27858
Phone: 1-252-847-6606

NORTH DAKOTA

Sanford Health Care
Myelodysplasia Clinic (pediatric and adult)
736 N. Broadway
Fargo, ND 58102
Phone: 1-701-234-6600

OHIO

Cincinnati Children's Hospital
The Center for Spina Bifida (pediatric-will refer adults)
3333 Burnet Ave.
Cincinnati, OH 45229
Phone: 1-513-636-4649
Phone: 1-513-636-8059
Web: www.cincinnatichildrens.org/

MetroHealth Medical Center
Comprehensive Care Program/Spina Bifida Clinic (pediatric and adult)
2500 Metro Health Dr.
Cleveland, OH 44109-1998
Phone: 1-216-778-5198

Rainbow Babies & Children's Hospital/University Hospitals Case Medical Center Pediatric Neuromuscular Rehab. Center (pediatric and adult)
11100 Euclid Ave., Mailstop: RBC 6081
Cleveland, OH 44106
Phone: 1-216-844-3597
Web: www.uhhospitals.org

Nationwide Children's Hospital Myelomeningocele Clinic (pediatric-will refer adults)
700 Children's Dr.
Columbus, OH 43205
Phone: 1-614-722-5725
Email:
victoria.hobensack@nationwidechildrens.org

Dayton Children's Hospital Myelomeningocele Clinic (pediatric-will refer adults)
One Children's Plaza
Dayton, OH 45404
Phone: 1-937-641-4073

St Vincent's Mercy Medical Myelomeningocele Clinic
2222 Cherry St., Ste. 2300
Toledo, OH 43608
Phone: 1-419-251-8008

OKLAHOMA

OU Children's Urology
1200 N. Phillips Avenue, 7th Floor, Suite 7100
Oklahoma City, OK 73104
Phone: 1-405-271 5458
Web: www.oumedicine.com/urology

OREGON

Child Development & Rehabilitation Center
Oregon Health & Science University (pediatric and adult)
Clinical Services Bldg
901 E. 18th Ave.
Eugene, OR 97403
Phone: 1-541-346-2606
Web: www.ohsu.edu/outreach/cdrc/

Doernbecher Chldren's Hospital
Child Development & Rehabilitation Center-Spina Bifida Program (pediatric and adult)
707 SW Gaines
Portland, OR 97239
Phone: 1-503-494-8085
Web: www.ohsu.edu/

Shriners Hospital Portland
Myelodysplasia Clinic (pediatric only)
3101 SW Sam Jackson Park Rd
Portland, OR 97206
Phone: 1-503-944-1169
Web: www.shrinershospitalsforchildren.org/

PENNSYLVANIA

Geisinger Medical Center (pediatric only)
Spina Bifida Clinic
100 N. Academy Ave.
Danville, PA 17822
Phone: 1-570-271-8055
Web: www.geisinger.org

Shriners Hospital for Children-Erie
Spina Bifida Clinic (pediatric to age 21)
1645 W. 8th St.
Erie, PA 16435
Phone: 1-800-873-8700
Email: sbirkmire@shrinenet.org
 Web:www.shrinershospitalsforchildren.org

Penn State Hershey Medical Center
Spina Bifida Services (pediatric and adult)
30 Hope Dr, ECO 20 or P.O. Box 859
Hershey, PA 17033-0859
Phone: 1-814-531-7522
Web: www.pennstatehershey.org/

Children's Hospital of Philadelphia
Spina Bifida Program (pediatric and adult)
34th and Civic Center Blvd.
Philadelphia, PA 19104
Phone: 1-215--590-1760
Web: www.chop.edu/service/spina-bifida-program

Moss Rehabilitation Center for Adults
Adult Spina Bifida Clinic (adult only)
60 Township Line Rd.
Elkins Park, PA 19027
Phone: 1-215-663-6677
Web: www.einstein.edu/

Shriners Hospital for Children
3551 N. Broad St., 4th Floor (pediatric only)
Philadelphia, PA 19140
Phone: 1-215-430-4028

St. Christopher's Hospital for Children
Spina Bifida Clinic (pediatric only)
Erie Ave. and Front St.
Philadelphia, PA 19134-1095
Phone: 1-215-427-5531
Web: www.stchristophershospital.com

Children's Hospital of Pittsburgh of UPMC
**Spina Bifida Department (pediatric to age
22)**
1 Children's Hospital Dr.
4401 Penn Ave.
Pittsburgh, PA 15224
Phone: 1-412-692-5096
Web: www.chp.edu

University of Pittsburgh Medical Center
UPMC Mercy PM&R Office
Adult Spina Bifida Clinic-Adult SB and
PM&R (adult only)
1400 Locust St., Building D, Ste. G103
Pittsburgh, PA 15219
Phone: 1-412-232-8903
Phone: 1-877-647-3438
Web: www.upmc.edu

RHODE ISLAND

Rhode Island Hospital/Hasbro (pediatric
only)
Children's Neurodevelopment Center,
Spina Bifida Program
593 Eddy St.
Providence, RI 02903
Phone: 1-401-444-3686
Web: www.lifespan.org/rih/

SOUTH CAROLINA

Medical University of South Carolina
Spina Bifida Program & Clinic (pediatric
and adult)
135 Rutledge Ave., Rm. 412
Charleston, SC 29425
Phone: 1-843-792-9895

Shriners Hospital for Children
950 W. Faris Rd (pediatric only)
Greenville, SC 29605
Phone: 1-864-255-7842
Email: jbrown@shrinenet.org

SOUTH DAKOTA

Please check neighboring states.

TENNESSEE

T.C Thompson Children's Hospital
Walter E. Boehm Birth Defects Center
(pediatric and adult)
975 E. Third St.
Chattanooga, TN 37403
Phone: 1-423-778-2222
Email: susan@boehmbdc.com
Web: www.boehmbdc.com

Children's Hospital Rehabilitation Center
1025 Children's Way (pediatric -no SB clinic. Only
P.T., Speech, O.T.)
Knoxville, TN 37922
Phone: 1-865-690-8961
Web: www.etch.com

Le Bonheur Children's Medical Center Spina Bifida Clinic (pediatric only)

50 N. Dunlap St.
Memphis, TN 38103
Phone: 1-901-287-6314
Web: www.lebonheur.org

Vanderbilt Children's Hospital Spina Bifida Program / The Junior League Fetal Center at Vanderbilt (pediatric - will refer adults)

11103 Doctor's Office Tower
2200 Children's Way
Nashville, TN 37232-9080
Phone: 1-800-526-4299
Phone: 1-615-343 4673
Web: www.vanderbiltchildrens.com

TEXAS

Dell Children's Medical Center of Central Texas Specialty Care Center (pediatric-will refer adults)

4900 Mueller Blvd.
Austin, TX 78723
Phone: 1-512-324-0137
Web: www.childrenshospital.com

Moody Clinic

1901 E. 22nd St. (pediatric only)
Brownsville, TX 78521
Phone: 1-956-542-8504
Web: www.moodyclinic.org

Texas Scottish Rite Hospital for Children Successful Bridges, Spina Bifida Clinic (pediatric)
2222 Welborn St.
Dallas, TX 75081
Phone: 1-214-559-7855
Web: www.tsrhc.org

Texas Tech Orthopaedic Clinic (pediatric and adult orthopaedic only)
4801 Alberta
El Paso, TX 79905

Cook Children's Medical Center Department of Neurology (pediatric-will refer adults)
901 Seventh Ave, Ste. 120
Fort Worth, TX 76104
Phone: 1-817-810-2500
Web: www.cookchildrens.org

Shriners Hospital for Children Myelo Program (pediatric only)
6977 Main St.
Houston, TX 77030
Phone: 1-713-797-1616

Texas Children's Hospital Spina Bifida Clinic (pediatric will refer adults)
6701 Fannin Street, Ste 1610.01
Houston, TX 77030
Phone: 1-832-822-4308
Web: www.texaschildrens.org

Wilford Hall Medical Ctr. Department of Urology (pediatric and adult)
2200 Berquiest Dr., Suite 1
Lackland AFB, TX 78236-5300
Phone: 1-210-292-5767

Christus Santa Rosa Center for Children and Families Spina Bifida Evaluation Center
333 N. Santa Rosa
San Antonio, TX 78207
Phone: 1-210-704-2335, ask for SB clinic
Phone: 1-210-704-2963
Email: Patricia.solis@christushealth.org

Methodist Children's Hospital Pediatric Specialty Clinics (pediatric only)
4499 Medical Drive Sublevel 1 @ Methodist Plaza
San Antonio, TX 78229
Phone: 1-800-297-1021
Web: www.mhshealth.com

UTAH

Primary Children's Medical Center
Spina Bifida Clinic (pediatric only to age 21)
100 N. Mario Capecchi Dr.
Salt Lake City, UT 84103
Phone: 1-801-662-1687
Web: www.ihc.com

Shriners Hospital for Children
Spina Bifida Clinic (pediatric only)
Fairfax Rd. at Virginia St.
Salt Lake City, UT 84103
Phone: 1-801-536-3564

VERMONT

Please check neighboring states.

VIRGINIA

University of Virginia
Kluge Children's Rehabilitation Center (pediatric only)
2270 Ivy Road
Charlottesville, VA 22908
Phone: 1-800-627-8596
Web: www.healthsystem.virginia.edu/internet/

INOVA (pediatric only)
8505 Arlington Blvd., Ste 100
Fairfax, VA 22039
Phone: 1-703-970-2685

Children's Hospital of the King's Daughters Spina Bifida Program (pediatric, will refer adults)
601 Children's Lane,
Norfolk, VA 23507
Phone: 1-757-668-9021
Web: www.chkd.org/Services/SpinaBifida/

Children's Hospital of Richmond Spina Bifida Program
2924 Brook Rd.
Richmond, VA 23220
Phone: 1-804-228-5818
Phone: 1-804-321-7474
Phone: 1-800-443-0893
Web: www.childrenshosp-richmond.org

WASHINGTON, D.C.

See District of Columbia above.

WASHINGTON STATE

Children's Hospital and Regional Medical Center Neurodevelopmental & Birth Defects Clinics (pediatric-will refer adults)
4800 Sandpoint Way NE
Seattle, WA 98105
Phone: 1-206-987-2184
Web: www.seattlechildrens.org

Spina Bifida Association of America (SBAA)
4590 MacArhur Blvd. NW # 250
Washington, DC 20007-4226
Phone: 1-800-621-3141
Phone: 1-202-944-3285
Web: http://www.sbaa.org

Shriners Hospital for Children Myelodysplasia Clinic (pediatric only)
911 W. 5th Ave.
Spokane, WA 99201
Phone: 1-509-623-0443

WEST VIRGINIA

West Virginia University Medical Center
Children With Special Health Care Needs/Myelo
Clinic (pediatric and adult)
Medical Center Drive
Morgantown, WV 26505
Phone: 1-304-598-4830

WISCONSIN

Gunderson Lutheran Spina Bifida Clinic (pediatric only)
1900 South Avenue
LaCrosse, WI 54601
Phone: 1-608-775 2169
Web: www.gundluth.org

American Family Children's Hospital Pediatric Spina Bifida Clinic (pediatric-will refer adults)
1675 Highland Ave.
Madison, WI 53792
Phone: 1-608-263-6420
Phone: 1-800-323-8942
Web: www.uwhealth.org

Children's Hospital of Wisconsin Spina Bifida Program (pediatric-will refer adults)
9000 W. Wisconsin Ave.
Milwaukee, WI 53201
Phone: 1-414-266-2690
Web: www.chw.org

Marshfield Clinic (pediatric and adult)
1000 N. Oak Ave.
Marshfield, WI 54449
Phone: 1-800-782-8581

WYOMING

Please check neighboring states.

OTHER IMPORTANT RESOURCES

Spina Bifida Health Care Benefits
P.O. Box 469065
Denver, CO 80246-9065
Phone: 1-888-820-1756
Fax: 1-303-331-7807
Email: www.va.gov/hac/contact
Web: www.va.gov/hac

World Arnold Chiari Malformation (ACM) Association
31 Newtown Woods Road
Newtown Square, PA 19073
Phone: 1-610-353-4737
Web: http:/www.pressenter.com/wacma/

Latex Allergy Links
Web Only: http//www.latexallergylinks.org/

Orthopedics Shriners Hospital
2900 Rocky Point Dr.
Tampa, FL 33607-1460
Phone: 1-813-281-0300
Web: http://www.shriners.com

Learning Disabilities Association of American
4156 Library Rd.
Pittsburg, PA 15234
Phone: 1-412-341-1515
Web: http://www.ldanatl.org/

Learning Disabilities Association of Canada
250 City Centre Avenue, Suite 616
Ottawa, Ontario K1R 6KT
Phone: 1-613-238-5721
FAX: 1-613-235-5391
Email: information@ldac-taac.ca
Web: http://www.ldac-taac.ca/

National Center for Learning Disabilities
381 Park Avenue South; Suite 1401
New York, NY 10016
Phone: 1-212-545-7510
Phone: 1-888-575-7373
Web: http://www.ncld.org/

Hydrocephalus Foundation, Inc. (HyFI)
910 Rear Broadway
Saugus, Massachusetts 01906
Phone: 1-781-942-1161
Web: http://www.hydrocephalus.org/

Spina Bifida and Hydrocephalus Association of Canada
#977-167 Lombard Avenue
Winnipeg, Manitoba, Canada R3B 043
Phone: 1-204-925-3650
Phone: 1-800-565-9488
Email: info@sbhac.com
Web: http://www.sbhac.ca/

International Federation for Spina Bifida and Hydrocephalus
Cellebroersstraat 16; B-1000 Brussels; Belgium
Email: info@ifglobal.org
Web: www.ifglobal.org

Guardians of Hydroccephalus Research Foundation
2618 Avenue Z
Brooklyn, NY 11235
Phone: 1-718-743-4473
Web: htt://ghrf.homestead.com/ghrf.html

National Hydrocephalus Foundation
12413 Centralia Rd.
Lakewood, CA 90715-1653
Phone: 1-888-857-3434
Email: hydrobrat@earthlink.net
Web: htt://www.nhfonline.org/

Hyrdrocephalus Association
870 Market Street, Suite 955
San Francisco, CA 94102
Phone: 1-415-732-7040
Phone: 1-888-598-3789
Email: info@hydroassoc.org
Web: http://www.hydroassoc.org/

The Sibling Support Project
Children's Hospital and Medical Center
PO box 5371 CL-09
Seattle, WA 98105
Phone: 1-206-368-4911
Web:
http://www.chmc.org/department/sibsupp/

Sibling Support Project
Don Meyer, Director
6512 23rd Ave NW, #213
Seattle, WA 98117
Phone: 1-206-297-6368
Email: donmeyer@siblingsupport.org
Web: http://www.siblingsupport.org/

National Father's Network
16120 N.E. 8th Street
Bellevue, WA 98008-3937
Phone: 1-425-747-4004 ext. 4286
Email: greg.schell@kindering.org
Web: http://www.fathersnetwork.org/

Mothers United for Moral Support (MUMS)
Phone: 1-920-336-5333
Web: http://www.netnet.net/mums/

National Parent to Parent Support and Information System (NPPSIS)
Phone: 1-706-374-6250
Web: http://www.nppsis.org

Manufactures for helpful devices for mobility and function:

Adaptive Mall.com
Bergeron Health Care
15 South Second St.
Dolgeville, NY 13329
Phone: 1-800-371-2778
Web: www.adaptiivemall.com

Prime Engineering
4202 Sierra Madre
Fresno, CA 93722
Phone: 1-559-276-0991
Phone: 1-800-827-8263
Web: www.primeengineering.com

Cascade Dafo, Inc.
1360 Sunset Avenue
Ferndale, WA 98248
Phone: 1-800-848-7332
Web: www.dafo.com

Rifton Equipment
PO Box 260
Rifton, NY 12471-0260
Web: www.rifton.com

One Invacare Way
Elyria, OH 44035
Phone: 1-440-329-6000
Web: www.invacare.com

SouthwestMedical.com, LLC
505 W. Thomas Road
Phoenix, AZ 85013
Phone: 1-800-236-4215
Web: www.quickie-wheelchairs.com

Online Support Group: for people interested in the care of children with Spina BifidaSB-Parents: send message to listserv@waisman.wisc.edu

(In body of email write "Subscribe sb-parents", then write your email address)

Bowel and Bladder Continence Supply and Vendors

180 Medical
6000 NW 2nd St. Ste 200
Oklahoma City, OK 73127
Phone: 1-887-688-2729
Web: www.180medical.com

Achieve Comfort Medical Equip. & Supply
370 S Fairfax Ave
Phone: 1-323-852-6900
Phone: 1-800-517-2477
Phone: 1-323-852-6904
Web: www.achievecomfortmed.com

Heartline Medical
PO Box 55
Hampstead, North Carolina28443
Phone: 1-866-791-4261
Web: www.heartlinemedical.com

Home Care Together
2536 Plover Road, Suite One
Plover, WI 54467
Phone: www.homecaretogether.com

Advocate Medical Services, Inc.
1202 Tech Blvd. #105
Tampa, FL 33619
Phone: 1-813-623-1028
Phone: 1-877-968-7267
Email: Juliov@advocatemed.com
Web: www.advocatedmed.com

Kleins Othopaedic and Medical Supplies
2015 State Rd.
CuyogaFalls, OH 44223
Phone: 1-330-926-5949
Enterostomal therapist on-site: Sally Thompson
Web: www.sthompson@kleinsrx.com

CCS Medical
2105 Newpoint Place Suite 600
Lawrenceville, GA 30043
Phone: 1-888-724-4357
Web: www.ccsmed.com

Southwest Medical
513 W. Thomas Road
Phoenix, AZ 85013
Phone: 1-800-236-4215
Phone: 1-602-230-9493
Fax: 1-602-279-0952
Web: www.southwestmedical.com

Express Medical Supply, INC
218 Seebold Spur
Fenton, MO 63026
Phone: 1-800-633-2139
Fax: 1-800-633-9188
Web: www.exmed.net

UTI Medical
579 Ravine View Dr.
Akron, OH 44303
Phone: 1-877-786-7884

EveryDay Medical
1139 Fulton Street, Suite 814
New York, NY 10038
Phone: 1-800-963-0633
Web: www.everydaymedical.com

UroMed
1095 Windward Ridge Pkwy. , Suite 170
Alpharetta, GA 30005
Phone: 1-800-841-1233
Phone: 1-678-356-0188
Phone: 1-800-208-0021
Web: www.uromed.com

References:

www.SpinabifidaAssociation.org

www.Mayoclinic.com

www.cdc.gov

https://www.indi.ie/diseases,-allergies-and-
medical-coditions/disability/385-diet-and-spina-
bifida.html

The McCormick Family

12 Years Old

About The Author

First time author Kenida McCormick was born in Blytheville, AK. She currently lives in Hope Mills, NC. with her husband and four kids. Singing is one of her hobbies. She also enjoys watching movies and TV series. Her favorite author is Dr. Seuss and her favorite song artist is Fantasia Burrino. When it comes to achieving her goals, Kenida is dedicated and very hard working.

Despite the different obstacles Kenida has encountered in life, she perseveres and keep working towards her dreams. She desires to one day be able to grant the dreams of special needs children as a way to give back to her community. Kenida's future is bright as she keeps her strong faith and remembers what is truly important in life.

In Kenida's free time she love to go out to eat at Chili's with her husband, sing karaoke and play rock band with her kids.

Made in the USA
Middletown, DE
17 August 2017